Preface

This volume contains the transcript of five taped interviews with Rear Admiral Daniel V. Gallery, USN (Ret.). They were obtained by John T. Mason, Jr. for the Oral History program of the U. S. Naval Institute. The interviews were held at various times between 1970 and 1974.

In the final interview the Admiral provides a summary of his writings. He is well known for his timely and often controversial remarks about naval matters - but whatever the subject there is present unfailingly a sparkling sense of humor to enliven the text.

Admiral Gallery's career in World War II is notable for his initiative in developing night operations from his jeep carrier in the Atlantic - and for the actual capture of German Submarine and crew. Gallery's ship towed the submarine to Bermuda where it was turned over to naval authorities. It is now a part of a museum exhibit in Chicago, the Admiral's native city.

A subject index has been added for convenience. Several interesting documents are a part of an appendix - including the famous Gallery Memorandum.

John T. Mason, Jr.
U. S. Naval Institute
Annapolis, Maryland

June, 1976

Reminiscences
of
Rear Admiral Daniel V. Gallery
U. S. Navy (Retired)

U. S. Naval Institute
Annapolis, Maryland

June 1976

DECLARATION OF TRUST

The undersigned does hereby appoint and designate as his (her) Trustee herein, the Secretary-Treasurer and Publisher of the United States Naval Institute to perform and discharge the following duties, powers, and privileges in connection with the possession and use of a certain taped interview between the undersigned and the Oral History Department of the United States Naval Institute.

1. Classification of Transcript.

   (✓) a. If classified OPEN, the transcript(s) may be read or the recording(s) audited by the qualified personnel upon presentation of proper credentials, as determined by the Secretary-Treasurer of the U. S. Naval Institute.

   ( ) b. If classified PERMISSION REQUIRED TO CITE OR QUOTE, the user will be required to obtain permission in writing from the interviewee prior to quoting or citing from either the transcript(s) or the recording(s).

   ( ) c. If classified PERMISSION REQUIRED, permission must be obtained in writing from the interviewee before the transcribed interview(s) can be examined or the tape recording(s) audited.

   ( ) d. If classified CLOSED, the transcribed interview(s) and the tape recording(s) will be sealed until a time specified by the interviewee. This may be until the death of the interviewee or for any specified number of years.

It is expressly understood that in giving this authorization, I am in no way precluded from placing such restrictions as I may desire upon use of the interview at any time during my lifetime, nor does this authorization in any way affect my rights to the copyright of my literary expressions that may be contained in the interview.

Witness my hand and seal this _____ day of Jan 29 1975

D. V. Gallery

I hereby accept and consent to the foregoing Declaration of Trust and the powers therein conferred upon me as Trustee:

R H E Bowen

classified as open
D.V.G.

REAR ADMIRAL DANIEL V. GALLERY

UNITED STATES NAVY, RETIRED

Born in Chicago, Illinois, on July 10, 1901, Daniel Vincent Gallery attended St. Ignatius High School in Chicago prior to his appointment in 1917 to the U. S. Naval Academy. As a Midshipman he was a member of the U. S. Olympic wrestling team and participated in the Olympic Games of 1920 held in Antwerp, Belgium.

Graduated in 1920 with the Class of 1921, he had duties afloat until 1927, when he was ordered to the Naval Air Station, Pensacola, Florida, for flight training. He received his "wings" as a Naval Aviator later that year. He was the Commanding Officer at the U. S. Navy Fleet Air Base in Iceland when World War II began, following which he took command of the "baby flattop" GUADALCANAL. He staged the first boarding and capture at sea of an enemy naval vessel since 1815 - the capture of the German submarine U-505 off Cape Blanco, French West Africa in June 1944. In 1955 his U-boat was brought to Chicago, hauled out of the water and installed on concrete cradles alongside the Museum of Science and Industry, as a memorial to the Americans who have lost their lives defending the country at sea.

He assumed command of the USS HANCOCK in 1945, in time to be present during the surrender ceremonies in Tokyo Bay. Following operational duty in the Pacific, he became Assistant Chief of Naval Operations (Guided Missiles) serving from 1946 to 1949. He hoisted his flag on the CORAL SEA as Commander Carrier Division SIX on March 10, 1951, and became Commander Hunter-Killer Force on March 21, 1952.

He commanded the nationwide Naval Air Reserve Training Command, headquartered at the Naval Air Station, Glenview, Illinois, between November 18, 1952 and November 1955, serving additionally from October 1954 as Commandant, Ninth Naval District, Great Lakes, Illinois. On December 6, 1956 he assumed command of the Caribbean Sea Frontier with additional duty as Commandant of the Tenth Naval District, with headquarters in San Juan, Puerto Rico. While in San Juan he was Commissioner of Little League Baseball for Latin America, and also organized the Tenth Naval District Steel Band (also known as "Admiral Dan's Pandemaniacs"), which has played on instruments made out of oil drums at the World Fairs in Brussels and New York. From May 17, to August 1957 he was assigned additionally as Commandant of the Fifteenth Naval District and from October 23, 1957 had further additional duty as Commander Antilles Defense Command. He served briefly in the Bureau of Naval Personnel,

Navy Department, prior to his retirement, effective October 1, 1960.

Rear Admiral Gallery has over 6,000 hours flying time in all types of Naval Aircraft, including single-seat jets and he is the proud holder of the "green" card issued to specially qualified instrument pilots by the Navy. His hobbies are baseball and writing. His writings have appeared periodically in the Saturday Evening Post and Colliers. He has written three books "Clear the Decks," "Twenty Million Tons Under the Sea," and "Now Hear This."

Rear Admiral Gallery has two brothers in the Navy, Rear Admiral William O. Gallery, USN, Retired, and Rear Admiral Philip D. Gallery, USN, Retired. Another brother, Reverend J. I. Gallery, pastor of St. Christina's Parish in Chicago, is a Naval Reserve Chaplain.

REAR ADMIRAL DANIEL VINCENT GALLERY
UNITED STATES NAVY, RETIRED

PERSONAL DATA:

Born: Chicago, Illinois, 10 July 1901
Parents: Daniel V. and Mary Onahan Gallery (both deceased)
Wife: Vera Lee Dunn of Fremont, Nebraska, married 9 August 1929
Children: James J., Beatrice C., Daniel V. Gallery, III
Official address: Harmony Farm Route #2, Vienna, Virginia
Education: St. Ignatius High School, Chicago, Illinois; U. S. Naval Academy, Annapolis, Maryland (BS, 1920, Class of 1921); Naval Air Station, Pensacola, Florida (Designated Naval Aviator 1927); Post Graduate School, Naval Academy (1932-1935 aviation ordnance); completed course in chemical warfare; completed Naval War College correspondence course in strategy and tactics.

PROMOTIONS:

Commissioned Ensign, 5 June 1920
Lieutenant (jg), 5 June 1923
Lieutenant, 5 June 1926
Lieutenant Commander, 30 June 1936
Commander, 16 August 1940
Captain (T), 21 September 1942
Rear Admiral (T), 10 December 1945
Captain, 7 August 1947
Rear Admiral, 1 August 1948, to rank from February 1944
Retired, 1 October 1960

DECORATIONS AND MEDALS:

Distinguished Service Medal
Bronze Star Medal
Presidential Unit Citation (Anti-Submarine Task Group 22.3)
World War I Victory Medal, Atlantic Fleet Clasp
American Defense Service Medal, Base Clasp
European African-Middle Eastern Campaign Medal with three bronze stars
American Campaign Medal
Asiatic-Pacific Campaign Medal
World War II Victory Medal
Navy Occupation Service Medal, Asia Clasp
National Defense Service Medal
Commander of the Britishe Empire (Honorary)
Expert Pistol Shot Medal

R. Adm. D. V. Gallery, USN, Ret.

CITATIONS:

Distinguished Service Medal: "For exceptionally meritorious and distinguished service to the Government of the United States in a duty of great responsibility as Commander of an Atlantic Fleet Anti-Submarine Task Group from January 4 to June 22, 1944. By his judicious planning and sound tactical judgment in selecting the most strategic localities for his task force searches...(he) enabled his highly efficient, expertly trained command to achieve unparalleled success against the enemy. Maintaining the group in a constant state of alert preparedness for combat and skillfully utilizing every available method of attack throughout the entire series of search patrols, he directed the operations of the task force aggressively and with brilliant initiative, relentlessly seeking out and inflicting tremendous damage on the hostile vessels..."

Bronze Star Medal: "For meritorious achievement as Commanding Officer, Fleet Air Base, Iceland, from December 1941, to May 1943...(He) organized and supervised the establishment and development of facilities for basing and supporting squadrons engaged in long-range anti-submarine patrol and convoy coverage missions. In spite of extremely adverse weather conditions, he rendered invaluable service in handling problems of adequate living conditions for personnel and aided in enlarging and improving facilities for the maintenance, repair, beaching and arming of aircraft..."

Presidential Unit Citation to Anti-Submarine Task Group Twenty-Two Point Three (USS GUADALCANAL, flagship): "For extraordinary heroism in action against an enemy German submarine during the capture of that vessel off French West Africa, June 4, 1944...The Units of Task Group 22.3 ...(forced) the U-boat to the surface...(boarded) the vessel while she was still circling...plunged through the conning tower hatch and worked desperately to keep her afloat and to aid other more fully equiped salvage parties in making the U-505 seaworthy for the long tow across the Atlantic...accomplishing the first successful boarding and capture of an enemy man o'war on the high seas by the United States Navy since 1915..."

CHRONOLOGICAL TRANSCRIPT OF SERVICE:

Jul 1920	Sep 1920	USS FREDERICK (in connection with Olympic Games, Antwerp)
Nov 1920	Jun 1921	USS DELAWARE
Jun 1921	Aug 1921	USS HERNDON (Special instruction in engineering)
Aug 1921	Aug 1922	USS STEVENS
Aug 1922	Jan 1924	USS PITTSBURGH (Engineering)
Jan 1924	Apr 1924	USS COLORADO
Apr 1924	Jun 1924	U. S. Naval Academy, Annapolis, Maryland (Duties in connection with Olympic Games)
Jun 1924	Dec 1924	USS RAPPAHANNOCK
Dec 1924	Jan 1927	USS IDAHO
Jan 1927	Nov 1927	Naval Air Station, Pensacola, Florida (flight training)

R. Adm. D. V. Gallery, USN, Ret.

Nov 1927	May 1930	Torpedo Squadron 9
May 1930	Jun 1932	NAS, Pensacola, Fla. (Instructor)
Jul 1932	Mar 1934	Naval Academy, Annapolis, Maryland (student in ordnance engineering)
Mar 1934	May 1935	Navy Yard, Washington, D. C. (continued instruction)
Jun 1935	Jun 1937	Scouting Squadron 4 (Commanding Officer from June 1936)
Jun 1937	May 1938	Observation Squadron 3 (CO)
Jun 1938	Jan 1941	Bureau of Ordnance (Head, Aviation Ordnance Section)
Jan 1941	May 1941	American Embassy, London, England (Ass't Naval Attache & Ass't Naval Attache for Air)
May 1941	Oct 1941	Staff, Commander Support Force, London
Oct 1941	Dec 1941	American Embassy, London (Special Naval Observer, Air)
Jan 1942	May 1943	Patrol Plane Base Detachment, Iceland (Commander)
Jul 1943	Sep 1944	USS GUADALCANAL (CO)
Sep 1944	Jun 1945	Office of Deputy Chief of Naval Operations (Air), Navy Dept.
Jun 1945	Dec 1945	USS HANCOCK (CO)
Dec 1945	Nov 1946	Commander Carrier Division 15
Nov 1946	Nov 1949	Office of CNO (Ass't for Guided Missiles)
Nov 1949	Sep 1950	Operational Development Force, Atlantic Fleet (Deputy Commander)
Sep 1950	Mar 1951	Commander Fleet Air Quonset, Quonset Point, Rhode Island
Mar 1951	Jan 1952	Commander Carrier Division 6
Jan 1952	Nov 1952	Commander Hunter-Killer Force, Atlantic
Nov 1952	Dec 1956	Naval Air Reserve Training Command, headquarters at NAS, Glenview, Ill. (Commander) with ADDU as Commandant Ninth Naval District, Great Lakes, Ill. from Oct. 1954
Dec 1956		Commander Caribbean Sea Frontier, ADDU as Commandant, Tenth Naval District, San Juan, Puerto Rico; as Commandant, 15th ND (May-Aug 1957); as Commander Antilles Defense Command (from Oct 1957)
Jul 1960		Bureau of Naval Personnel, Navy Dept.
Aug 1960		Hospitalized
1 Oct 1960		Retired

Navy Office of Information
Internal Relations Division (OI-430)
9 December 1964

Rear Admiral Daniel V. Gallery

U.S. Naval Institute

Annapolis, Maryland

August 19, 1970

By: John T. Mason, Jr.

Mr. Mason: Admiral Gallery, I'm delighted that you will do a series based on your highly interesting and successful naval career. I wonder if you would begin in the usual way by telling me the date of your birth, the place of your birth, something about your family background, and certainly include something as to how two brothers in addition to yourself made the Navy a career, how this came out of your family background, things of that sort, your early education.

Admiral Gallery: I was born July 10th, 1901 in Chicago. My father's name was Daniel V. Gallery (I'm junior) and my mother was Mary Onahan Gallery. All of my grandparents, except one, were born in Ireland and came over to this country around 1845.

Q: During the potato famine in Ireland. It was a great exodus of people at that time.

Gallery: Yes, that's right.

My mother's mother was born in Boston, but her ancestry was also Irish. So all four of my grandparents were Irish.

Q: Did they come directly to the middle west when they came?

Gallery: Yes. My grandfather Onahan, whom I knew better than any of the others, my mother's father, came there as a young man. I think he was about 20 when he got to Chicago about 1845. I remember him saying that when he first came to Chicago he knew everyone he'd meet on the street. He saw that city grow from around thirty thousand to three and a half million in his life time.

I went to school at St. Patrick's Academy and St. Malachi's parochial school, and then to St. Ignatius High School, a Jesuit high school, for two and a half years. Then I dropped out to prep for the Naval Academy.

Q: Tell me something about that time. Had you any intention of preparing for a naval career or did your family have other thoughts for you? What kind of a student were you?

Gallery. It was all very simple. This was settled for me by my dad. I had no choice whatever in the matter.

He just decided I was going to the Naval Academy and that was it.

Q: What made him arrive at such a decision? What was his business?

Gallery: He wanted to go to the Naval Academy himself, but when he was young he lost an eye so he couldn't. He sort of realized his own ambition by sending three of his sons to the Academy.

Q: What was his business?

Gallery: He was a lawyer.

We three had no choice whatever in the matter. The old man decided that we were going to the Naval Academy and that was that. In my opinion, this is the way it should be worked. It's fine. I've been grateful to him ever since.

Q: Very few examples of that kind of authority today.

Gallery: Incidentally, there were four brothers in the family. Three of us eventually turned out to be Rear Admirals. The other one went straight, he's a priest.

Q: He's a priest in the church. Was this also your

father's intention, that he should become a priest?

Gallery: My father and mother sort of agreed on that. The priest is named John Ireland. He's named after Archbishop Ireland, who was his godfather and a great friend of my grandfather Onahan. He was designated from the day he was born to be a priest, as the rest of us were to be naval officers.

Q: This was very often true with a staunch church family. That one child was designated for the church. Whether it be, in case of a girl, for a convent or for a boy, priesthood.

What gave your father such a strong interest in the Navy?

Gallery: I never knew. I don't know just what it was, but I know he wanted to go to the Naval Academy himself. When he couldn't go, he sent his three sons.

Q: There was no objection on your part? You just went along with what the parent decreed?

Gallery: Oh, you didn't object to what the old man wanted, you went along. It was a little different in those days from what it is now.

Q: What kind of a student were you at St. Ignatius?

Gallery: I was a pretty sharp student. I led my class all the time I was there.

I was appointed to the Naval Academy by Congressman Gallagher, who was our regular Congressman, and took the entrance exam in the Federal Building in Chicago and passed.

I entered the Academy in August of 1917. I wasn't 16 until July 10th of that year, so I wasn't eligible to enter until I was 16. I was not quite the class baby. My class, at that time, was the largest that ever entered the Academy. I think we had 650.

Q: This was because of the on-coming war?

Gallery: The war was in progress then. That was the reason for the expansion, of course.

We had 650 in the class. I think I was fourth or fifth from the class baby. There were three or four younger than I was, but not many.

Q: Did you have to go to one of the Prep Schools here in Annapolis?

Gallery: No. I took private tutoring in Armour Institute

in Chicago.

The Jesuit high schools didn't go in very much for mathematics. They went in for Latin and Greek, and that sort of stuff. So in order to pass the entrance exam in mathematics, I had to take private tutoring which I took at Armour.

I entered the Academy here in August, 1917 and was sworn in by Rear Admiral Eberle. I remember the duty officer the day I reported in was an officer by the name of Lieutenant Commander William F. Halsey, who later went on to bigger and better things.

Q: How did you take to the discipline and the life at the Academy?

Gallery: I took to it all right, it didn't bother me a bit. I fitted right in.

At that time they were just building, what we called, the new wings on Bancroft Hall, the third and fourth wings. They weren't finished yet. So on account of the tremendous expansion, they didn't have room enough for everybody in Bancroft Hall. They put a large number of the new plebe class over in the Marine barracks over on the other side of College Creek. I was one of the so-called barracks plebes. We were over there all by ourselves.

I spent plebe year over there. Then the new wings were finished and we moved in to Bancroft Hall.

I was a pretty good student. In the class of 650, my final standing on graduation was 54 I believe.

Q: Indeed you were. How many graduated out of that large number?

Gallery: Out of 650: At that time it was a three year course. They had cut the time on account of World War I. Then the war ended while we were still Midshipmen, so they had to go back to the four year classes. So they cut my class in two. One half graduated in three years, and the other half in four years. Everybody in the first half graduated in three years, and I was in the first half.

I graduated in 1920, although my class is '21.

In athletics, I was on the wrestling squad. I was just a little bit of a kid, skinny as a rail, and growing, shooting up like a weed. In my first year, I wrestled bantam weight, 115 pounds. First class year, I had to move up to the next weight, 125 pounds. I was quite a good wrestler, I won every bout. In my first class year, I won all my bouts by falls.

I graduated in 1920. That was the year of the Olympic Games in Antwerp. So I went on to the Olympics in wrestling.

Q: That's where Weems was too, wasn't it?

Gallery: That's right. That's where I got to know Mammy.

At the time I was shooting up like a weed, and I grew out of the 125 pound class. I had to wrestle light weight at the Olympics.

Q: If you'd kept on you'd have become a heavy weight.

Gallery: Yes. The trouble was I could step on the scales and weigh in as a light weight with my clothes on, and that's no good. Because the guys you're going to wrestle have taken on maybe ten pounds to make the weight.

Anyway, I didn't do too well in the Olympics. I met a Finn there who was just a little too much for me to handle. I did beat a Belgian and a Dane and got to the quarter finals, but that was as far as I got in the Olympics.

There is one thing that happened while I was a Midshipman that maybe is worth relating here. I had a fist fight with the Secretary of the Navy's son. Josephus Daniels was the Secretary of the Navy and his son was Worth Bagley Daniels.

Right after the armistice Worth Bagley resigned. There were a lot of comments made about this lad resigning right after the armistice was signed. I was one of those who made these comments, which I think now were completely unjustified. But anyway, there were a lot of derogatory comments made and young Daniels challenged me to a fist fight.

I told him I would fight him with gloves in the gym, because the regulations at the time specified that fist fights between Midshipmen were a kick-out offense. So I said, "I'll fight you with gloves in the gym." He said no, he didn't want that, he wanted a bare fist fight. So then I told him, "If you'll wait until your resignation is accepted, you'll be a civilian and I'll be a Midshipman, and I'll fight you then." That was not covered by regulations. So we left it that way.

It took about two weeks for his resignation to go through.

Q: Was he your relative size?

Gallery: During those two weeks, I had a very bad two weeks because he was a welter weight at the time and I was a bantam weight. He was the class behind me. People kept coming around me and telling me, "This guy is a real battler. He was the welter weight champion of his class." I'd never done anything but a little alley fighting when I was growing up, so I figure I'm just due for a hell of shellacking here, but there isn't any way of getting out of it, so that's that.

Finally his resignation went through after about two weeks. The day it was accepted, he came up to my quarters after third period recitation. We shoved the chairs and table out of the way. My roommate, Cootie Koops, stood watch outside the door for the duty officer.

Q: They had never gotten wind of this?

Gallery: No.

Then we went to it, with bare fists, just the two of us in the room. As I said, I was fully prepared to take one hell of a shellacking. As soon as the fight started, I made the amazing discovery that this lad was a sucker for a straight left. Every time I poked my left hand out, I hit him right on the nose. After four or five minutes, all this time I was just jabbing with my left hand, finally I uncorked a right that caught him right on the button and knocked him out. That was that.

When he came to, we shook hands, and that was that. He shoved off.

That happened about five minutes of four, when the fight finished. Drill call went at four o'clock. So I had to clean up and change clothes and so forth, and just barely made it down for formation for drill. When you're in drill, you're all busy, you're not supposed to talk to each other and so on. But I would say in the hour of drill, the news of that fight spread to everybody in the Naval Academy. I'd never seen the news spread so fast, everybody knew about it. By the time drill was over, everybody knew about it.

The next morning the Baltimore and Washington and New York newspapers had the story on their front page. Not my name, my name was not mentioned. But it was the story of the son of the Secretary of the Navy beating up this big bully who had been picking on him while he was a Midshipman, quite a dramatic story. That was Sunday.

Monday morning when I came back from first period recitation, there was a note on my desk, "The Commandant wants to see you." That was W. H. Standley.

Whenever the Commandant sent for you, it was something real serious. I knew what this was, of course. I figured, "This is the end of my naval career. I'll be on the way out the main gate before lunch."

I went down to Admiral Standley's office and he was sitting there with the morning papers on his desk. He said, "Young man, I understand you are the Midshipman involved in this story." I said, Yes, sir." He said, "Well, tell me the story." I was so sure the jig was up

Gallery #1 - 12

and I was going out by lunch time, I just told him the story the way I'm telling it to you now. I didn't try to gild the lily or anything, I just let him have it. When I got through, old Standley sat there. He had a paper cutter in his hand, tapping on the paper. I sort of expected him to take the paper cutter and run it into me any minute. He sat there tapping for quite a while without saying anything. Finally he said, "Well, Mr. Gallery, your conduct was entirely blameless. You may go."

Ever since that time, I've regarded Admiral Standley as one of the greatest naval strategists of modern times.

I guess he didn't like Josephus Daniels very much. There were a lot of officers about this time who didn't, you know.

That was one of my high spots in my career as a Midshipman.

Q: Were you deprived of the ordinary type cruises during the summer during your period there then?

Gallery: Youngster cruise we made in Chesapeake Bay, in the old, old battleships. There was the Maine, Missouri, and Ohio. We spent the whole summer in Chesapeake Bay.

First class cruise, the next year, the war was over by then. We were then split up in small groups and sent

Gallery #1 - 13

to the battleships of the Atlantic Fleet. I spent a month and a half in the New Mexico and a month in the Oklahoma.

Q: But you didn't get to Europe or anything of that sort?

Gallery: Oh, no. The New Mexico was in New York, and never left New York. The Oklahoma was in Norfolk, and never left there. There was no real cruise at all.

Q: But still you got to see what it was to be on board ship and be a real sea-going sailor. You liked the idea?

Gallery: Oh yes, sure.
   I accepted right from the beginning that this was what my life was going to be and that was that. I never questioned it.

Q: Were your two brothers in the Academy at the same time?

Gallery: No. Bill came along in the class of '25. I was a year out by that time. Phil was class of '28. Bill and Phil were together here for a year, but they weren't here while I was here.

Q: What was your particular interest as you went through

the course here? What aspect of naval service seemed to appeal most?

Gallery: I'd say my main interest was in athletics. Of course, I was quite successful with wrestling. I took part in class baseball. I was too small for football, or crew, or anything of that kind.

I never had any particular difficulty scholastically.

Q: Did you show any aptitude at that time for writing and so forth?

Gallery: No. As I remember, my grades in English were about 3.2 or 3.3, just below star mark in those days. I don't know what star mark is now, it used to be 3.4. No, I didn't show any aptitude for writing.

The course had been cut then to three years.

Q: What was eliminated in order to make it a shorter course?

Gallery: That's going back a long way. I can't say that I remember, I don't know.

Q: Were there foreign language requirements?

Gallery: Yes, you had a choice of either French or Spanish.

As I understand it, they have a great number of optional courses here now. There were not in those days, except for either French or Spanish. That was the only optional we had.

Q: Was there any interest, at that early date, in aviation at the Academy? Was there anything that pointed in that direction?

Gallery: No, I didn't have any particular interest in it at that time. Aviation was just in it's very early infancy then. My interest in aviation didn't awaken until four or five years after graduation.

Q: What did you do immediately following your graduation? What kind of an assignment did you get?

Gallery: The first assignment was the U.S. Olympic team.
Then the USS Delaware, where I was in the engineers. I was in the Delaware for a year, and then went to destroyers, where I was chief engineer of a destroyer with a fifty percent crew. This was during the cut back after World War I.

Q: It was awfully difficult to get recruits, too.

Gallery: That's right.

I was in the Stevens, a little four pipe destroyer for a year. Then put her out of commission up in the Philadelphia yard and went to the USS Pittsburgh, which was one of the old armoured cruisers and then went to Europe. I was in the Mediterranean, we went there in '22 I believe, '22, '23, and part of '24.

Q: On what ship?

Gallery: On the Pittsburgh.

Q: What kind of duties did she have there in the Med?

Gallery: We got there just as Kemal was running over Asia Minor, and threatening to take Constantinople. So the Pittsburgh was sent to Constantinople. At that time, there was probably the largest international fleet that had ever been assembled was right there in Istanbul. Every nation which had a navy had heavy representation right there in the Bosporous. The allies were still occupying Constantinople. There was an army of occupation of several hundred thousand there. There were perhaps half a million Russian refugees, the cream of Czarist Russia, who had escaped the revolution were there. We had this international fleet, the army of occupation, and the Russian refugees. Everybody figured, "Drink and be merry for tomorrow Kemal comes and that's the end of everything."

I wouldn't say Istanbul was a hotbed of Christian virtue at the time. It was quite a hot place.

Q: I guess rarely it is.

Gallery: I think we were at Istanbul about eight months.

Q: We had an admiral there, did we not? Were you on his staff then?

Gallery: Admiral Bristol, yes. No, I was an ensign then on the Pittsburgh. Bristol, of course, was ashore. He was actually the American Ambassador. Then we had another admiral on the Pittsburgh, Long.

While we were there it was touch and go very often as to whether Kemal was going to actually move on Constantinople, or whether there'd be another war down there. In fact, at times it was a very close thing. But eventually the war business blew over and Kemal settled in Asia Minor, and the capital moved to Ankara, and things quieted down. So then we left, the Pittsburgh left Istanbul and we started cruising.

We went all through the Med, all around Europe, and

up into the Baltic. We stopped practically everywhere where the port had deep enough water for us.

Q: That was really showing the flag, wasn't it?

Gallery: Just showing the flag, yes. That was really prime duty for a young ensign.

Q: A grand tour. Did you have a good skipper on the Pittsburgh?

Gallery: Yes, we had J. V. Kleman.

After about a year and a half on the Pittsburgh, I was ordered back to the states. That took us up to 1924.

I was ordered back to the Academy here to train for the 1924 Olympics, as a wrestler. I tried out, but I didn't make it.

So then I went out to the west coast and joined the battleship Idaho. I had turret one on the Idaho for a little over a year.

On all the ships that I was on up to that time, I always had charge of the ship's wrestling squad and developed some darn good wrestlers for fleet champs.

On the Idaho, I was also editor of the ship's paper, which was my first, you might say, literary endeavor.

Q: How did you happen to get that job?

Gallery: I don't recall now just how I did get it. At any rate, I became editor of the ship's paper and ran a darn good ship's paper too, if I do say so myself. I occasionally got in a little difficulty doing that.

One time, for instance, we were scheduled to go into Seattle for the week-end. At the last minute the orders were changed and we were sent to Anacortes, Washington, which is just a little bit of a fishing village on Puget Sound. This was a hell of a come down for the whole crew who'd been looking forward to a big weekend in Seattle, one of the big ports in the country, to have to spend the weekend in Anacortes. It was quite a come down, and everybody was feeling pretty teed-off about it. So, as editor of the ship's paper, I decided to a little funny paper to maybe help the morale of the boys. So we put out an issue of the paper which was devoted to the history of Anacortes, but it was all a lot of phony stuff that we made up out of thin air. The villain of this piece was the Mayor of Anacortes. I m sure if I had let some competent attorney look at that issue of the paper before we put it out, he would have said no, he'll sue you for a million bucks for this thing. But anyway, we put out this issue of the paper, history of Anacortes.

The day that we went in and anchored at Anacortes, the Mayor came out to call on the Captain and offered him the keys to the city. Just as the Mayor and Captain sat down in the cabin for a cup of coffee, a Marine orderly walked in with two issues of the Idaho Yarn right hot off the press, and handed them to the Captain. The Captain saw the headline, "History of Anacortes," so he very proudly handed the thing to the Mayor. The Mayor took one look at the damn thing and immediately got up on his feet and walked out. The Captain and the Mayor went up to the gangway and the Mayor shoved off. The Captain then sent for me.

I was fired as editor of the ship's paper then and there, but I got the job back the next day because after all I was putting out a pretty good ship's paper. I was a little more careful about what I said about the Mayors of towns that we were going to visit from then on.

While I was in the Idaho, I got the flying bug.

Q: And how did you get that?

Gallery: Everybody was getting it along about that time. Practically all of the junior officers along about my time who were eligible wanted to go flying, and I was one of them.

Incidentally, our exec was A. B. Cook, who eventually retired as Vice Admiral. As junior officers we would put in for aviation, the request would go through the exec. He used to get each one of us in there and give us a lecture about giving up our birthright for a mess of pottage. This was one of the watch words of the ship, "Your birth right for a mess of pottage." and a lot of us gave it up.

Then by golly about a year after I learned to fly who should show up down at Pensacola to learn to fly himself but A. B. Cook, giving up his birth right for a mess of pottage, too.

From the <u>Idaho</u>, I went to Pensacola. I got there in 1926. It was from January of '27 until September I was at Pensacola. I had a little trouble to begin with. I busted my first solo checks and for a while thought I wasn't going to make it, but eventually I passed the solo check. I went on with no trouble from then on. As a matter of fact, I stood number one in the fighter plane course at the end of the course.

Q: Tell me a little about the course set up as it was at that time at Pensacola.

Gallery: You started off then flying seaplanes. Of course, we don't have any seaplanes in the Navy any more.

Q: You didn't have any glider experience?

Gallery #1 - 22

Gallery: No, no glider. We started off with seaplanes. We flew the old N-9, which was a Jenny really with an extra wing section put in and a pontoon on it. Then after going through the course in seaplanes, you shifted to land planes. The primary trainers were the NYs. That was all just the primary training stuff.

Then you went to the so-called advanced training, which at that time was still at Pensacola. Then you learned to fly observation planes, big boats, and fighters. As I recall it, the course ran around 300 hours flying time then. Then you got your wings, and went out in the fleet.

Q: Were there a great number of casualties during the training period?

Gallery: In my class, we had as I remember 25. Incidentally, one of those 25 was Captain E. J. King.

Q: Some of the older officers went down there about that time.

Gallery: Actually in my class we had King, Kelly Turner, Bernard, and Alford. They were the four senior ones in the class. Alford was a Lieutenant Commander, Bernard and Turner were Commanders, and King was a Captain.

Then we had about ten sailors, APs. We had the AP rating then.

In my class we had about 30. We had two killed during the course in collisions, McCord and Frawley.

The first year after we finished Pensacola, as I recall it, we had six killed. From then on, we only lost one. That was Hopping, shot down by the Japs during the war.

That was sort of the history of most classes along about that time. In the first two years, you had pretty heavy casualties. Then those that got through the first two years made out pretty well.

Q: Did the older officers have any particular difficulty in going through the course?

Gallery: No, they didn't.

Admiral King, for instance, sailed right through. He was pretty old when he went through. In primary seaplanes, I remember, there was one part of the course where you had to do stunts. They told King that they would excuse him from the stunt check, on account of his age. King said, "Nothing doing. I'll take the stunt check the same as everyone else." And he did. He went right through.

Q: Do you have any other recollections of him as a flying

student in that time?

Gallery: He was a very austere and reserved sort of character. For the first month or so, while he was around down there living in the BOQ with the rest of us, nobody could get friendly with him at all. But then after about a month, he loosened up and he became one of the boys.

Then after we had finished the course and gotten our wings and went back in the fleet, he became E. J. King again.

Q: What was this, a conscious effort at reserve or was it a natural thing?

Gallery: It was just his natural way, that's all. We did manage to get under his hide and loosen him up while he was a student.

I got to know him pretty well later on. I must say I always got along pretty well with him.

Q: Of course at that point there was a considerable difference in rank, and I suppose that was a factor.

Gallery: Oh yes. He was a captain and I was a lieutenant.

I got my wings in '27. I finished one in the fighter

course. Of course everybody wanted to be a fighter pilot. Instead of that, I was sent to Torpedo Squadron nine, which was sort of a bastard outfit. We were flying Tams, which was a carrier based torpedo plane but they had put pontoons on this thing. (We were in Norfolk). So we were a torpedo plane squadron on pontoons.

We operated up and down the east coast, down as far as Panama and back, and then down to Guantanamo for the winters.

We never got near a carrier, because we had pontoons. And we weren't really a patrol squadron, because this twin pontoon was just a make shift. If you ever had to land in rough water, it was a crackup. It was just a smooth water operation.

Q: It was in effect coastal defense, was it?

Gallery: Well, yes. We were trying to be a patrol squadron. Our cruise and radius was about 500 miles. We operated from little tenders like the Sandpiper and the Teel. They would go on ahead of us down the coast and anchor and put out buoys for us. Then we'd come along and tie up to the buoys and spend the night on the Sandpiper or the Teel.

We trained in horizontal bombing and dropping torpedoes. However, the torpedoes we had at the time were very primitive. They were what we started World War II with. You had to get down practically touching the water to drop your torpedo. In fact, when you dropped your torpedo unless you felt a splash come up and hit your tail, you were too high and you were apt to damage the thing.

Contrast that with the Japs, who dropped them about 150 feet at high speed. The Jap torpedo would run shallow. Our torpedoes would go out and take a deep dive, and they'd stick in the mud unless you had a lot of water.

We thought, for that reason, that our battleships were safe in Pearl Harbor. We thought if the Japs dropped any torpedoes they'd stick in the mud. The Japs had torpedoes that didn't take a deep dive. We didn't have those kind.

Q: Did you have the actual warheads as you went on these flights along the coast?

Gallery: We just had exercise heads. Usually we were dropping dummy torpedoes, wooden torpedoes.

Q: That was another lack, wasn't it, the use of dummy torpedoes in the place of real ones?

Gallery: Yes. There were a great number of things wrong with our torpedoes that we didn't find out until the war started. We started firing them at ships and the explosives didn't work and that sort of thing. That's another story and we didn't have much to do with that then.

Q: How closely did the Bureau of Aeronautics keep in touch with this squadron?

Gallery: Pretty closely, the Bureau of Aeronautics did. Those were the days of the brown shoe and the black shoe Navy. God damn aviators was a hyphenated word. But the Bureau of Aeronautics took care of its own people.

We operated up and down the coast to Panama, to Guantanamo, and Media Luna Cay. We came up here to the Naval Academy for the summer to fly the Midshipmen around. I was up here for two summers doing that.

Q: So you were beginning to make an impression on the whole Navy.

Gallery: From there I went to Pensacola as an instructor. I was down there for about a year and a half. This was 1930, '31.

Q: Was there any noticeable change in facilities and in

Gallery #1 - 28

techniques and so forth at Pensacola when you went back as an instructor?

Gallery: No, I wouldn't say any great change from the time I was there as a student. Except that the place was expanding all the time and getting bigger and better outlying fields, and things of that kind. We were still using the same sort of planes and the same general course of training.

Then from Pensacola I went to the P. G. School through aviation ordnance. That was over here in the Marine barracks at that time.

I put in three years in aviation ordnance and became a member of the so-called gun club then.

Q: Did you go to MIT also?

Gallery: No. Aviation ordnance was a year and a half here at the P. G. School and then a year and a half circulating around from the Proving Ground at Dahlgren, Ford Instrument Company, the Norden Company, the Gun Factory, and places of that kind.

Q: Did that end with a graduate's degree?

Gallery: No, we didn't get any degree, except membership

in the gun club which at that time was supposed to insure a long and successful naval career.

Q: Being tapped for P. G. School usually did, didn't it?

Gallery: Yes. Incidentally, I was way late in going to the P. G. School. This was 1931 or 2, which was ten years after graduation.

Q: Yes, that's an unusually long time. Did it entail any difficulties for you, in terms of studying?

Gallery: No, it didn't. I had no particular difficulty and did very well at the P. G. School.

Q: What was the particular interest in that course, and in your exposure at Dahlgren and Norden and so forth?

Gallery: My main interest of course was aviation ordnance. I became interested in bomb sights and also in anti-aircraft directors and that sort of thing.

I went from the P. G. School to VS Squadron Four, which was a scouting squadron on the old Langley. The first year there I was operations officer. Then the second year I was fleeted up to command of that squadron. We operated off the Langley, the Ranger, the Saratoga, and the Lexington.

Then I went from that to VO three, which was a battleship squadron, back with the <u>Idaho</u>. I was in the <u>Idaho</u> for a year on Admiral Wainwright's staff as his senior aviator and the squadron commander.

Q: Is there anything particular in that tour of duty that should be noted?

Gallery: It was just the usual sort of thing: training around North Island, and cruises in the carriers, and participating in fleet problems.

Q: Did you get involved in any of the war games in the Pacific?

Gallery: Yes, each year they had their war games and we participated in them.

Then from battleships I came to duty in Washington in the Bureau of Ordnance as officer in charge of the aviation section. I relieved Malcolm Schoeffel in that job. Schoeffel, incidentally, had relieved Forrest Sherman, who eventually got to be CNO.

Q: This entailed close cooperation with Bureau of Aeronautics when you were there.

Gallery: Yes.

The major effort of my section was concerned with the Norden bomb sight. When I took over, our commitments with the Norden Company were around $800,000 a year. By the time I left, which was about two years later, we were committed to something like $80,000,000 a year with the Norden Company.

Q: That bespeaks your special interest in bomb sights.

Gallery: Of course, the Norden Bomb Sight was a very fine instrument for the purpose for which it was designed, which was to bomb a moving ship target. And it was the best instrument that had been designed up to that time for that sort of a target.

It turned out that the Air Force wanted the Norden bomb sight. When the tremendous expansion began, the Navy had to supply the Air Force with all their bomb sights, which was the reason for the tremendous expansion from $800,000 a year to $80,000,000.

The ironic part of it was: I haven't any idea how many millions we did put into the Norden bomb sight but it was a tremendous amount because every heavy bomber had one. And actually they were of no use to the Air Force because all their bombing was area bombing, lots of it at night, or you couldn't identify a point of aim. They were just bombing cities. A Norden bomb sight wasn't designed for that at all. It was of no use in that sort of warfare.

The Navy actually didn't use the Norden bomb sight because we found that dive bombing was much more accurate and much easier to train people for than horizontal bombing anyway.

Q: But it was one stage in the development, wasn't it?

Gallery: It was a stage that was a dead end. We never used it because dive bombing took over.

The only actual occasion when the Norden bomb sight was used, for the purpose for which it was built, was in dropping the two atom bombs on Hiroshima and Nagasaki. There they insisted on good weather where you could see and identify your target, and the point of aim was very carefully picked out so the bomber could actually put the cross hairs of his sight on a certain point on the ground and focus on it, synchronize on it, and use it as intended to put his ground zero of his bomb right smack where he wanted it. It did that in both Hiroshima and Nagasaki.

Those are the only two cases in the whole war in which the Norden bomb sight was used for the purpose for which it was built. And God knows how many millions we put into it.

Q: Did any other foreign navy have a counterpart to the Norden bomb sight at that point?

Gallery: No. We got several captured German sights from planes shot down over England and they sent the sight over here to us. I remember taking one of them home and taking the thing apart. It was nowhere comparable to the Norden sight at all.

As a matter of fact, in the sort of bombing that they were doing at that time there was no need for a precision sight. Because half the time on the night raids, for instance, they would frequently go out to bomb Hamburg. They would go out and drop their bombs and come back in and report that they had blasted hell out of Hamburg. Then a couple of days later they would discover instead of Hamburg it was maybe Dusseldorf or some other completely different town. Bombing in those days was very much hit or miss.

Q: That leads me to another question, in terms of ordnance in general. When you were there working on aviation ordnance, was there any free exchange of information with the Royal Navy?

Gallery: With the Royal Navy, yes, complete free exchange. Shortly after I got to the Bureau of Ordnance, the policy of complete cooperation with the British was in effect. I think the Norden bomb sight was the only thing we kept away from them.

Q: That must have been an awfully well kept secret, if the enemy didn't get hold of it.

Gallery: It was, very well kept.

Q: Did you take part in trial uses of it and so forth down at Dahlgren and other places?

Gallery: Yes. I had very close connections with the Norden Company, old man Norden himself and Ted Barth, who was his number two.

Q: What else did the Norden Company develop?

Gallery: That was it, that was all. They worked on dive bomb sights, but it was not successful.

Dive bombing, at that time, was a matter of getting practically directly over your target and then diving very steeply on it. You just used a telescope sight, aimed a little bit over the thing, and let go. At low altitude it was comparatively simple if you trained for it. You got pretty good accuracy from it.

Whereas, even using a Norden bomb sight, it took a lot of training to learn to make a good bombing run. To use a Norden sight, of course, you had to have a point of aim. And when you got into this business of aerial bombing and bombing cities at night, you had no point of aim.

Q: That was the saturation technique that they finally came to.

Gallery: That's right.

Q: What else in your BuOrd period was of interest? Anything in the area of gunnery?

Gallery: This was '39, '40, and '41 when I was in the Bureau of Ordnance. This was the time when we were making tremendous expansions in the Navy. We started building the two ocean Navy so our aviation activities were expanding quite rapidly at the time, along with the rest of the fleet.

We had our first real carriers come along. Of course, we did have the Ranger. Then the next was the Langley, the Lexington, the Saratoga, along with the Ranger.

Q: The Essex class was coming along then?

Gallery: No, the Essex class came a little later.

There were two in between. I've forgotten the names of these now. But we had a couple of true carriers built as carriers right from the beginning. Then the Essex class came along, quite a slew of them.

In the meantime, our aviation was expanding tremendously. My job in the Bureau of Ordnance was to provide the armament for the planes. This was expanding tremendously along with all the rest of the Navy.

Q: This must have involved some real application at shipyards and other places?

Gallery: Yes. We had a very busy section at the time. Of course, the whole Bureau was very busy.

When I came to the Bureau, that was in '39, this was right after the war had started.

Q: What were some of the particular problems that you encountered in this vast expansion?

Gallery: There were a lot of arguments between the Bureau of Aeronautics and the Bureau of Ordnance as to who supplied what. Then when we came to armour plating for airplanes, and leak proofing the tanks, these were things that we learned after the war started were necessary.

Then we were moving from 30 caliber guns to 50 caliber to 20 millimeter. That was it, outside of the tremendous expansion we had to make in production facilities for the Norden bomb sight.

Q: How much did you actually learn from the battle experiences of the British fliers? Did you have special emmisarries in London reporting directly to the BuOrd on this?

Gallery: We learned a lot.

Yes, as a matter of fact, I was just coming to my part of that. In 1941, in January, I went to London as a special observer. I was there for three months attached to the Embassy and circulating around among the various airfields in England and the fleet, observing.

At the end of that time, after three months there, I came back to the Bureau and was there just a very short time when I was detached and ordered back to England in connection with the building of the seaplane base at Loch Erne. This was late '41, about September.

We were building this big seaplane base in Loch Erne, looking forward to the time we were going to be in the war. This was all undercover at that time of course, because there was no assurance that we were going to be in it. We were building the seaplane base there and I was designated to be the commanding officer of it, when and if we got in the war. I was over there for about three months on that job.

Q: What was the anticipated role of the seaplanes?

Gallery: Taking part in escorting convoys in the battle of the Atlantic, which was one of the crucial battles of the war. At that time, we were losing the battle of the Atlantic hand over fist.

So we were building this big seaplane base. This job as skipper of that base was really one of the plums, especially for somebody of Commander rank which my rank was then. I was over there from September through December while the base was being built.

Q: How many seaplanes were to be accommodated by this base?

Gallery: We would have had about four squadrons.

As I say, this was a real elite job. But then the Japs came along and knocked the whole thing into a cocked hat with Pearl Harbor and they knocked me up to Iceland. Instead of having this nice plush seaplane base at Loch Erne, I left as commanding officer of the Fleet Air Base Iceland. Which was a hell of a come down because up in

Iceland, when I went up there we had nothing but a bunch of abandoned Nissen huts that the British had put up and eventually abandoned. Things were pretty primitive.

Q: Did the seaplanes fulfill the expectations, in terms of convoying?

Gallery: Yes, they were very useful indeed. Eventually they were replaced by the long range shore based airplane. But at the beginning of the war, we didn't have those kind of airplanes. The seaplanes played a very important role.

Up in Iceland, eventually, I had a squadron of PBY's, the old work horse, PBY amphibians. We were escorting convoys past Iceland. We'd go out for 13 hour hops and pick the convoys up 500 miles south of Iceland, and escort them for three or four hours. If you'd pick them up at 500 miles it took you about five hours to get out there and five hours back, and that only left three or four hours.

Q: Were these U. K. convoys, or were they Murmansk run, or what?

Gallery: They were both, mostly U. K..

That brings us up to the point where we've gotten into the war. I think maybe we could stop there for this session.

Rear Admiral Daniel V. Gallery, USN

U. S. Naval Institute

Annapolis, Maryland

March 5, 1971

By: John T. Mason, Jr.

Mr. Mason: It's awfully good to see you this morning, Admiral. Last time you talked somewhat extensively about your early naval career. Your concluding remarks had to do with the assignment to set up a seaplane base in the United Kingdom, but events moved fast and we were catapulted into the war and so you got an assignment to go to Iceland. Would you tell me about that?

Admiral Gallery: It was quite a comedown for me, to go from this very fine seaplane base that we were building at Loch Erne, Scotland up to Iceland, where I became the Commanding Officer of the U. S. Navy Fleet Air Base, Reykjavik, Iceland.

When I got there the Fleet Air Base consisted of some Nissen huts that had been abandoned by the British, which our people had moved into. We had a squadron of PBY airplanes there and an old four-pipe destroyer in there to sort of act as tender for them. The boys were really roughing it there. Life was primitive, to say the least. But it was wartime and we'd just been knocked flat on our can at Pearl Harbor, so we were willing to put up with some hardships.

We were working very closely with the RAF and the Royal Navy. The mission of this squadron was to help escort the convoys going past Iceland. They were passing four to five hundred miles south of Iceland, and we would fly out and escort them as far as we could.

Q: These were convoys going to the U. K.?

Gallery: The U. K. and back.

A little later they were running convoys from Iceland to Murmansk, that came a little later.

For all practical purposes we were an RAF squadron. We worked very closely with the RAF and the Royal Navy.

Then when I arrived there we got to setting up our own Fleet Air Base, and that took several months. We had a Seabee outfit up there who built the base for us. They brought in Nissen huts and all the necessary galley and living equipment and that sort of thing.

Q: That must have been one of the early Seabee outfits, was it?

Gallery: It was, yes.

Inside of about three or four months we had a very

comfortable base up there, at least in comparison to what we had started with.

Q: That speaks well for the effectiveness of the Seabees, doesn't it?

Gallery: Those Seabees were a tremendous outfit, of course.

All the time I was there we had one squadron of PBY amphibians, and our job was helping escort convoys past Iceland.

Q: Was there much interference at that stage of the game on the part of the Germans?

Gallery: Oh boy, that was right at the height of the battle of the Atlantic, and the convoys were catching hell. So we had a busy time.

Some interesting and more or less humorous sidelights about that time - when I first showed up there and met the British Air Commodore and the British Rear Admiral, I noticed that they were both rather reserved in their reception of me. Then after I got to know them pretty well and saw that they had a twinkle in their eyes one of them remarked to me one day, he said, "We were rather suspicious of you when you first came up here to take command of this place because one look at your face, which is a map of Ireland, made us a bit suspicious that you might be rather difficult to get along with and that you might make things as difficult as possible for Her Majesty's forces."

So I told them - no, I had no feelings of that kind whatsoever. I said, "As a matter of fact, I bear no ill will whatever toward the British. As a matter of fact, I am eternally grateful to your ancestors for persecuting my ancestors so that I was born in the United States."

I had to exchange a lot of memos and correspondence with the Rear Admiral and the Air Commodore. Whenever you have any correspondence with a high ranking British officer, he signs his name and he puts a whole flock of initials behind it - D.S.O.K.C.B. and all that sort of thing indicating the orders and decorations that he had.

I had nothing to put behind my name except 'junior,' which made no impression whatever on our gallant allies. So after I got to know them better and saw the twinkle in their eyes, I began putting D.D.L.M. after my name, knowing very well that sooner or later one of them would ask me - what did it mean.

And sure enough one morning the Air Commodore met me in RAF headquarters and after saying, "Good morning, Dan old man," he said, "I say, old boy, what does that D.D.L.M. mean that you put after your name?"

I said, "Oh, that's the American equivalent of your K.C.B." (Knight Commander of the Bath is one of the biggest and best things they've got.) So the Air Commodore was duly impressed.

He said, "Oh that's splendid, that's fine. I didn't know you Americans had any such thing."

Then I could see the wheels going around inside his head, trying to figure out what they stood for and finally he gave up. He said, "Just what do the initials stand for?"

I said, "They stand for Dan, Dan the Lavatory Man, the same thing as K.C.B., isn't it?"

That was on the humorous side. The other side of it was rather grim, escorting of the convoys.

This was at the height of the battle of the Atlantic, when the Germans were sinking seven or eight hundred thousand tons a month. They were sinking ships faster than we could build them at that time, and we were sinking very few submarines.

And actually the fate of England was hanging in the balance at that time. There were times when England was within sight of starvation and surrender.

That went on through all of '42. I believe it was April of '43 that the tide suddenly turned. From that point on we were winning the battle of the Atlantic. Up to that point we'd been losing it.

The tide turned very suddenly and dramatically, and it was the result of four or five different things which all came to a head at once.

One was the tremendous building program in the United States. Another was the advent of long range aircraft, which could reach out into the middle of the Atlantic from shore bases which we couldn't do prior to that. Another was the advent of the jeep carrier, which closed the gap in the middle of the Atlantic. And there was a new radar and better depth charges and homing aircraft torpedoes.

All these things came to a head at once, and when they did we slaughtered the U-boats for three months - April, May, and June of '43, when we sank a hundred U-boats and just rocked the U-boat fleet right back on their heels. From that time on we were winning the battle of the Atlantic.

Q: In that early stage, how many ships would be in a convoy? And how many would be lost?

Gallery: Some of the convoys had a hundred ships. In some convoys we lost as many as twenty.

On the Murmansk run, which was a brutal thing, PQ-17 - we lost well over half of that. I'll never forget that.

The convoy before PQ-17 had been very roughly handled. And they had trouble with the crews of the merchant ships on PQ-13. They almost mutinied and weren't going to sail. But they promised them a tremendous naval escort, so they got them to sail. They sailed, and this naval escort that they were promised was the Washington and the K.G. V. They were supposed to protect the convoy.

Actually they tagged along about 150 miles astern of the convoy. The convoy came under attack by submarines and aircraft.

I remember very well on the fourth of July of that year I was in the RAF headquarters that morning, and we were looking at the chart showing where the convoy was. It was up around the North Cape of Norway, and it was having a bad time. We got a flash that the Tirpitz was coming out to attack the convoy.

The Air Commodore and I just rubbed our hands together and said, "Boy, this is it. The Washington and the K.G. V will get the Tirpitz today." I remember very well the Air Commodore rubbed his hands and he said to me, "Boy this looks like it's going to be the best fourth of July since you blokes declared your independence."

Then about an hour later we got this message from London, "All warships retired at high speed to the west, convoy scattered."

Everybody just slouched out of Air Force headquarters

and went back to their huts and either cursed or wept or both. That was the story of PQ-17. That convoy was slaughtered.

The reason behind that order from London was that our battleships had been catching hell along about that time. We had lost our whole fleet at Pearl Harbor. The Prince of Wales and the Repulse had been sunk at Singapore. All the shipyards were full of battleships which had been damaged by either air attack or torpedoes.

So the British were simply gun shy, and they weren't about to risk any more big ships within range of either torpedoes or aircraft. And so even though they had the word that the Tirpitz was coming out, they recalled the Washington and K.G. V and told them to retire to the east.

As a matter of fact when the Washington got back to Reykjavik after that, the boys didn't want to come ashore because they didn't want to face their friends there, after turning around and abandoning the convoy.

Q: Actually, the difficulty with those Murmansk convoys was more with the German planes, wasn't it, coming off the North Cape?

Gallery: It was both planes and submarines. Fortunately, the German air force and the German submarines didn't work together very well, fortunately for us. They worked more or less independently. Had they worked together on that Murmansk run, they would have stopped the run. But as it was they would both work on the same convoy, but with no cooperation between them.

Old Goering had no use for the German navy. He wouldn't give them any long range reconnaissance aircraft. He wanted to do the whole job himself. So he'd send his planes out and find a convoy, and then send his bombers out to get them. But he wouldn't tell the navy where the convoy was.

Q: I talked with Sam Frankel at great length about the Murmansk convoys, he being at the other end of the line. He's told me about the difficulty with the merchant seamen, and their difficulty in getting them to face those dangers and hardships.

Gallery: The Russians, incidentally, were always promising us that they would have tremendous air escort meet each Murmansk convoy at the North Cape and bring it all the way into Murmansk. And they never sent a damn thing out, nothing. But before each convoy they'd promise us all sorts of heavy air escort, which they never produced.

Q: They didn't really have it, did they?

Gallery #2 - 50

Gallery: I don't know whether they did or not, they claimed they did, and that they would supply it. But they never did.

Incidentally, Sam Frankel, who was up there at Murmansk, was a student of mine down at Pensacola.

Q: That must have been quite an assignment there in Iceland. Difficult, yes, but once the tide began to turn you must have felt a sense of accomplishment.

Gallery: Yes. It's a time that I look back on with no regrets whatever. It was rugged duty in a way, but in other ways it wasn't. And we could certainly feel that we were pulling our weight in the battle of the Atlantic.

We had one squadron of seaplanes up there, old PBYs, which could only make a hundred knots. But they were all right for anti-submarine work, 14 hours radius. True, when we would go out to escort a convoy that was passing 500 miles south of Iceland, it would take us five hours to get out and five hours to get back. We only had two hours on the convoy, because you had to have a couple hours spare gasoline to get back.

Anyway, we pulled our weight in the boat. We sank five or six subs, which was quite a respectable score for one squadron.

Q: Who was in command then of the North Atlantic -

Ingersoll?

Gallery: Ingersoll was Commander-in-Chief of the Atlantic. Admiral Bristol had the so-called Support Force, which was based in Newfoundland, and we came directly under Admiral Bristol.

Q: Did you get out of there at all during that time, or were you simply stationed in Reykjavik all that period?

Gallery: I was there the whole time. I did get back to Washington for about two days once, but that was all.

Q: What did you do for amusement, for a break in the routine there?

Gallery: We did all right. We had pretty good recreational facilities. We had a gymnasium there, rather it was a storehouse which we converted to a gymnasium. We played basketball. We had some red hot basketball games there with the Army. We had bowling alleys. We played a lot of softball. We had a lot of social activities with the local people - dances and that sort of thing.

Q: How were you received by the Icelanders?

Gallery: The Icelanders were rather cool to us, because they had been up there for about a thousand years minding their own business and keeping out of the world's wars and they didn't appreciate it when we muscled in on them.

Q: They were kind of provincial, weren't they, in their attitude?

Gallery: Call it that if you want to. They just wanted to be let alone, and we'd moved in on them. But after awhile they got used to it.

Incidentally, an interesting sidelight on our moving in - the Icelanders were very, very, poor people, most of them. That is by our standards anyway. Their annual income was way below our poverty level here, when we moved in. But they lived a fairly happy existance.

Then we moved in on them, and we started building camps and bases and things all over the island and spending all sorts of money there. So everybody in Iceland made a lot of money and wages went way up, and so did prices. With the result that nobody was a damn sight better off than they had been in the first place.

Now that's something for us to think about here in this country today.

Q: Do you want to comment on the effectiveness of the RAF, as you worked with them?

Gallery: The RAF Coastal Command was the outfit that I was working with, and they were extremely effective. Their main mission was escort of convoys, anti-submarine warfare. And they were damn good at it, and did a very fine job.

Q: You said that you got a new type of radar equipment along about '42. Had you had radar at the beginning?

Gallery: Yes, we had radar right from the beginning, but this was a very much improved type of radar.

Q: Was this a British type radar or was it American?

Gallery: I don't know. Radar developments at that time were a joint business, and we were both in it right up to our ears. So you could hardly say that any radar was British or American, it was a joint affair.

Q: I do know at the time of the battle of Britain, so-called, that was surely British.

Gallery: Yes, that was all British.
But then, of course, we got in it full scale after that.
The German submarine people were reluctant to believe

that it was possible for an airplane to carry a radar. For a long, long time they simple wouldn't believe it. Their radar experts told them that the necessary equipment for radar was too big and too heavy to put in an airplane. Doenitz kept heckling the radar experts on the subject, and that was their story for a long, long time - that it was simply impossible to do it.

But we had aircraft radar along about '43. By that time they realized we had radar, and they had rather primitive means for detecting our early radars.

Then we came out with a new short range, rather short wave, radar, which was very much improved, which they couldn't detect. For a long time we were catching their people on the surface, coming in on a radar approach. We'd catch them sound asleep on the surface.

This was one of the big developments of the war, as a matter of fact.

The German scientists misled their submarine people very badly on the subject of radar.

Q: That says in fact that their intelligence was not that good.

Gallery: Yes, that's right.

As a matter of fact, their submarines kept coming back in and reporting that aircraft had come down out of the clouds blind, just burst right out of the clouds, and attacked them. Obviously it was radar that was doing that. The submarine people kept telling this to their scientists. And the scientists kept saying, "It's impossible, they can't have aircraft radar."

Q: During your time there, did you capture any submarine crews?

Gallery: Yes, we captured one crew. As a matter of fact this was our first kill.

An interesting story in connection with that - after we'd been there several months, we had several chances for attacking subs and we muffed them for various reasons - one maybe buck fever on the part of the pilot, or maybe bomb rack hung up and didn't work, or various things of that kind. We missed our first three or four chances.

So I laid down the law to the boys and said, "From now on we're closing the bar in the officers club until we get a sure kill," which was a cruel and unusual punishment. Anyway, we closed the bar.

Then a couple of weeks later this lad, Hopgood, went out and caught a German sub and attacked it with depth charges and damaged it so that it could not submerge. Hopgood was on the way to a convoy, which was about a hundred miles from the spot where he attacked the sub. After he had expended all his depth charges, he then saw that the sub was surfacing and couldn't submerge. He then flew from that spot to the convoy and told them about the sub, and they broke off a couple of destroyers to go over and get the sub. He circled back and forth between the disabled sub and the oncoming destroyers, coaching them on.

The submarine came across an Icelandic fishing vessel. They went alongside the fishing vessel, and boarded it, abandoned the sub, opened the scudding valves on it, sank the sub, and headed for Germany with the fishing vessel.

Hopgood saw all of this, he was circling around reporting it to these destroyers, and they kept coming. Eventually they came alongside the Icelandic fishing vessel and went aboard and got the whole German crew and took them prisoners.

Of course, this was a very exciting time in all the RAF headquarters, while this was going on, because this report was coming in from out at sea. And so at all the RAF headquarters in England and up in Iceland the big wheels were gathered around the radio set listening to this very dramatic development out at sea.

All of Hopgood's reports of what was happening were framed in very official language and coded, of course. Everybody hung on each report as it came in.

Then at the end when the British destroyers took the Germans off the Icelandic fishing vessel, Hopgood's last report came in to me in plain English, no code, he said, "Sank sub, open club."

And we did, we damn near blew the roof off the joint. At the height of the celebration that night we decided that we needed a suitable trophy for this victory. So the most suitable trophy would be the skipper's pants - in other words we'd caught him with his pants down.

So I wrote a letter to the First Lord of the Admiralty, who had been up there and had addressed our officers about two weeks before. I wrote to him and explained the American expression, 'caught with your pants down,' and said, "We would like to have the skipper's pants to hang in the bar room of our officers club. In order to avoid leaving the skipper in an embarrassing position, I am sending herewith a pair of my own khaki pants which you can exchange with him for his."

I got a nice letter back from the First Lord of the Admiralty saying that he had turned my letter over to the proper authorities and I would be hearing from them before long.

About two weeks later I got a very stuffy letter from the head of naval intelligence quoting the Geneva Convention on the business of humiliating prisoners and so forth and so on. And he said, "In view of this, it is impossible to send you the skipper's pants."

I didn't mind the melarky about the Geneva Convention so much as I did the outrageous fact that he didn't even send my own pants back.

Q: Was any thing of value learned from these men, did you know?

Gallery: I don't know what they got from them when they got them to England. They put them through the usual questioning business.

While we were up in Iceland, of course, the German battleship, Tirpitz, was sort of hanging over our heads. It was up in one of the fiords of Norway, I don't remember exactly where, but it hung out in the Norwegian fiords. There was always a possibility that she would break out into the Atlantic the way the Bismark did.

Of course, I knew that if this ever happened she'd probably come through the Denmark Strait, north of Iceland. And I knew that some night in the middle of the night I'd be woken up and handed a message from London saying, "Tirpitz is going to pass through Denmark Strait, go get her."

We had a squadron of PBYs which could carry aircraft torpedoes. This is why I knew darn well that they would want us to go get her, on account of the torpedoes. But a squadron of PBYs against the Tirpitz would have been practically suicide, because they were so slow and the Tirpitz had a hell of a fine aircraft battery.

So if we went in by ourselves it would have just been suicide, but if we could put on a coordinated attack with the support of bombers and fighters at the same time, I figured that we might have a good chance of putting the Tirpitz on the bottom.

So I began agitating around Iceland with the RAF and the British navy to draw up plans and get us a task group ready in case the Tirpitz ever did try to make a break to get her. It took a lot of persuasion on my part to get them to take this thing seriously, but finally they did.

And we drew up a task organization in which we had the RAF, the U. S. Army Air Forces, and the U. S. Navy all formed into one task group, of which I was to be the O.T.C.. We were to put on a coordinated attack on the Tirpitz with fighters, bombers, and torpedo planes, all hitting at once.

Incidentally, when we got this plan drawn up, I took it around to the British Rear Admiral there for him to look at. When he looked at it he sort of frowned a bit and then he said, "Well, but the Tirpitz is CinC Home Fleet's bird." But I finally convinced him that if the CinC Home Fleet's bird ever got as far away from home as Iceland, it was up to us to get the bird. And he went along with it.

The plan was finally approved all up the line. We held several Tirpitz drills. In fact, whenever a British battleship came in to Iceland, we would have a Tirpitz drill. This task force would meet her and simulate the attack.

As a matter of fact, I found out later that Admiral King got a big bang out of my final plan for the attack, in which the last paragraph was a time schedule of events. As I remember it was something like this - with minus ten minutes fighter planes attack the Tirpitz, minus five minutes the bombers attack the Tirpitz, zero minutes the torpedo planes come in and attack, plus two minutes Tirpitz blows up and sinks. That was the end of the plan. Admiral King got a big bang out of that. But we never did get a shot at the Tirpitz.

Another interesting little sidelight on this thing was - after one of our Tirpitz drills, when K.G. V came in with the Commander-in-Chief Home Fleet on board, we met them and put on the attack and so on. Then afterwards the Air Commodore and the U. S. Army Air Force Colonel and I went out to the K.G. V to discuss this thing with the Commander-in-Chief.

When we were leaving the K.G. V, which was anchored up in Hvalfjordur, this was in the middle of January, bitterly cold, ice all over. They had side boys lined up, piping the whistle and all this and that, and we went down the gangway. They had a couple of sailors at the bottom of the gangway to help the big wheels get into the boat. As the boat was pulling away from the gangway, one of the British sailors slipped on the ice and plopped into the water just as the boatswain's mate was piping us away. His pals stood there at rigid attention with salute until the piping was finished, then they reached down to haul their friend out of the water.

I remarked to Rear Admiral Dalrymple-Hamilton, who was the British CinC Iceland, "Good show, you know traditions of Nelson," and all that sort of thing. He said, "Oh yes, I'm sure any one of your sailors would have done the same thing."

I just couldn't resist the temptation. I thanked him and I said, "Yes, but of course none of my sailors would have been clumsy enough to fall overboard."

Q: What was the time span that a man could stay in that icy water?

Gallery: About five minutes.

Q: This was a problem with our planes, was it not?

Gallery: Yes. When a plane went down, if the crew was in the water five to ten minutes that was the end of them. And the same thing with the ships in the convoys that were sunk.

Q: Was there any effort to create a life preserver that would be useful to guard against such frigid temperatures?

Gallery: No, if you were in the water for five to ten minutes the chances are you were finished.

Q: This only added to the peril of service there. Did this have any effect on the morale?

Gallery: No, this was just one of the hazards of the game that everybody knew about and accepted. There wasn't any thing we could do about it.

Q: Did you have any contact with the merchant crews, the American merchant seamen?

Gallery: No.

Q: I understand that many of them were of quite a radical turn of mind.

Gallery: They were. And we heard about it indirectly because the Murmansk convoys assembled at Hvalfjord which was up the fiord from Reykjavik about ten miles.

Q: That was a protected area, was it?

Gallery: Yes. But our air station was at Reykjavik itself, so we never saw the merchant sailors at all. But we heard about some of the troubles they had.

Q: When did you leave Reykjavik for service with the Guadalcanal, the baby flattop?

Gallery: I left Reykjavik I believe about the 1st of June of 1943.

Q: Just as the tide of battle was turning there.

Gallery: It had turned by then. April, May, and June was when we really broke the back of the U-boat fleet.

I came back to Washington then and had a month's leave here with my family.

Then I went out to Astoria, Oregon as prospective CO of the USS Guadalcanal, which was a Kaiser Class converted carrier, so-called jeep carrier. It was 11,000 tons built to merchant ship standards, and could make 19 knots. By all Navy standards these ships were just impossible, but actually they did a tremendous job in the war.

Q: The prototype for one of those baby flattops had been used in the North Atlantic, had it not? What was that?

Gallery: Yes. The Long Island I think was the very first one. It was a converted merchant ship.

Q: That's the one that Wu Duncan put in commission.

Gallery: That's right.

The Long Island and a number of others were converted merchant ships, and the British had some. Then Kaiser got in the business and he built sixty of them, I believe.

The Kaiser ships were not converted merchant ships. They were built right from the keel up as carriers, but they were built to merchant ship standards. They were just barely good enough, but they were good enough. And they did a tremendous job during the war in the Atlantic hunting submarines. There were only three or four of us that got into the Atlantic. The rest of them all went to the Pacific and they were used almost entirely for aircraft transports - that is hauling replacement planes for the fast carrier task force.

Q: What was the complement of planes on the Guadalcanal?

Gallery: On the Guadalcanal we had twelve TBMs - the so-called turkey Martin torpedo planes. And I believe we had eight single seater fighters - I forget what we used to call them. That was our complement - twelve torpedo planes and eight fighters.

I tried to get rid of the fighters and get other torpedo planes to replace them, but I never could sell that idea. The fighters were of no use to me at all. But they kept saying the Germans have got the Fokke-Wulfe, which was a very long range plane, which theoretically could get out more or less to a ship like the Guadalcanal. So they said we had to have the fighter planes to protect against the Fokke-Wulfe, but we never did encounter any Fokke-Wulfes.

We assembled the crew for the ship, while it was building at Astoria. We assembled the crew up at the Navy Yard, Puget Sound, where they went to the pre-commissioning school, while the ship was being built.

The building of the ship, incidentally was a complete innovation in the eyes of shipbuilding, inasmuch as up to that time each ship was built individually - you might say the way a fashionable tailor makes a suit of clothes, each suit of clothes is a little bit different.

In the case of the Kaiser Class carriers, these were mass produced the same way automobiles were. Very large sections of the ship were built in various parts of the country and shipped to Astoria, where they were put on an assembly line. They'd assemble these sections on the building ways and weld them together, and then slide the thing down the waves and into the water.

Q: I suppose this was the first time that kind of technique was employed in building ships.

Gallery: That's right, yes, the first time.

There were also some wild rumors going around at the time that these ships were defectively designed, and that they would break in two as soon as they got into a heavy seaway. There were a couple of the C-4 cargo ships that broke in two, which lends a little weight to this thing. I remember I had to get my crew together and assure them that there was no truth to this whatsoever.

Although I remember very well the first night that we got underway, when we left Astoria. The very first night, it was rougher than hell that day. The ship was bucking and pitching. All along the hanger deck there were very thin plates, which had nothing whatsoever to do with the strength of the ship. They were really just spray shields. But as the ship would sag over the top of a wave, and then hog and sag, these plates would oil can in and out. That noise just boomed through the ship like thunder, and it sounded like we were just about to break in two any minute. I'm sure that everybody on the ship thought of this business of breaking in two that night, but it didn't.

Q: What sort of a complement of men did you have?

Gallery: I believe we had twelve hundred men. I would say of that twelve hundred, maybe a thousand were on their first ship. They were absolutely green.

Then we had perhaps two hundred who had had experience on other ships. Some of them came from carriers which had been sunk in the Pacific, we had one or two of them. It was a completely green and inexperienced crew.

Q: You had no time for a shakedown?

Gallery: We had a shakedown of sorts. We went from Astoria around to Norfolk. You might say that was our shakedown cruise.

In a way having a completely inexperienced crew like that has some advantages. One of them was that I had very high ambitions for this ship. So I was proposing the boys right from the start that we do some things that to an old timer would sound a little far fetched. In fact, an old timer might say, "Well, this skipper is nuts. You just can't do this." But with a bunch of completely inexperienced kids they said, "Well, if the old man says we can do it, we can." By God, they went out and did it.

One of the things was this business of towing a submarine home, which I had in mind right from the beginning. Incidentally, that idea originated in a way up in Iceland. I forgot to mention that in the Iceland business, but this was right after Hopgood's exploit - where this sub was surfaced and crippled.

Discussing that around the fireplace in the officers club one night we got to letting our imagination run riot, and we said, "Why couldn't we board and capture a submarine with a PBY aircraft?" You could land a PBY in fairly rough water, you could not get it off again, but you could land it.

The idea would be that we'd crippled this guy and force him to surface. And when we'd come along and we'd land right close to him. We'd taxi up and put one wing over the deck, throw grappling hooks over him and get hold of him.

Meantime, we'd have our machine guns peppering away at the conning tower to keep people down below. And we'd get a couple of people over into the sub, and run up to the conning tower and heave a hand grenade down there to let them know we really mean business. Then we'd throw a chain down so that they can't close the conning tower hatch and submarge. And then we'd get possession of the thing.

We've got a plane in the water we can't get off, but anyway we've got the sub and we know he can't submerge. So then we'd send a message in to the base and tell them, "We have captured a sub, send out and get it."

Along about that time by the time we got that far in the planning it was about one o'clock in the morning and we all decided to go to bed and sleep it off. So that was that.

But this was really where the idea of capturing a sub started - up there in Iceland. And I still had it in the back of my mind when we were putting the Guadalcanal in commission.

As a matter of fact, on our shakedown cruise I had one of the exercises which we ran through, this wasn't on our regular schedule of exercises but I wanted to do it anyway, was to take a destroyer in tow. Which was a very laborious job handling those heavy lines and so on, and the boys didn't like it a damn bit. But anyway, we did take a destroyer in tow. I didn't say that the thing I had in mind here was eventually taking a U-boat in tow, but that's what I did have in mind.

This gets back to an inexperienced crew at times being an advantage, because they'll believe a lot of things that a bunch of old timers wouldn't believe. They'll not only believe them, they'll go out and do them.

Q: But it makes the task more formidable to commission the ship and have a lot of green horns on board.

Gallery: Among other things, to get away with a program like that, you've got to be lucky. And we were a lucky ship right from the beginning.

Q: When you commissioned her, did you know that your destination was to be the Atlantic?

Gallery: No, we thought we were going to the Pacific.

When I got the word we were going to the Atlantic, I was bitterly disappointed because I figured I'd done my stint in the Atlantic and that the battle of the Atlantic was won now anyway. So I figured we were just going to backwater the war now, and we ought to be going to the Pacific.

I squawked about it, but it didn't do any good. So we had to go to the Atlantic. And, of course, it was the biggest break that I ever got when we did go to the Atlantic.

On our shakedown cruise we went first to San Diego, where we picked up our air group and spent some time breaking them in. Incidentally, I made the first take-off and landing from the ship in an SNJ down at San Diego. The reason why I wanted to do that was I had rather ambitious plans for the air group, too. And I wanted the people in the air group to know the skipper could do these things himself as well as talk about them, so I made the first landing and take-off.

Q: Good idea. Were they experienced men?

Gallery: No, they believed what I told them, too. This was one of the reasons I wanted to make the first landing and take-off, to add credibility to what I was telling them.

One of the big things that we did, from many points of view, more difficult than capturing that submarine, was we broke the ice in the Atlantic on night flying. I'll come to that later.

We left San Diego and went down through Panama to

Norfolk. On the way to Panama we had a war game with the air defenses of the Panama Canal. About a week before we got there, we got this message requesting that we stage a mock attack on the Canal. So we did.

There were two ships that went down together - the Mission Bay and the Guadalcanal. I was the Task Group Commander.

What we did on this attack was we put all our fighter planes on the Mission Bay and all our torpedo planes or bombers on the Guadalcanal. We shifted them at sea on the way down.

When we got within two days cruising of Panama, we split up. The Mission Bay proceeded to Panama, and we doubled back and came up near the coast of Nicaragua.

The next morning the Mission Bay launched all her fighters, had them climb up to about 20,000 feet and then head in for Panama, knowing that the Panamanian radars would pick them up high up in the air and hoping that they would send all the defending fighters out to attack this group coming in. Which was exactly what they did.

Meantime, we were up in Nicaragua and we launched our bombers. They flew across Nicaragua and then down the Panamanian coast on the Atlantic side. And they came in from the Atlantic side and caught them absolutely flatfooted.

That was quite a business, because they sent everything

out to attack the <u>Mission Bay</u>, which came in from the Pacific.

Q: So the Canal was destroyed - somebody else had his pants down.

Gallery: We caught them with their pants down on that all right.

Q: In order to do that, did you have to notify the Nicaraguan government?

Gallery: I think we should have, but we didn't.

Q: They were at war, too, weren't they?

Gallery: I don't remember now.
    Anyway, we just flew across the isthmus and came down the Atlantic side.

Q: How effective was the radar protection for the Canal, that would be toward the end of '42?

Gallery: They spotted our fighters coming in from the Pacific, where they expected us to come from. They spotted them and they went out and intercepted them.

But they weren't looking the other way, and our bombers came in undetected.

We got up to Norfolk around Christmas time, and we shoved off on our first cruise early in January.

Q: Would that be escorting a convoy?

Gallery: No.

The way they worked it at that time was you would sail about the same time as a convoy did, but you were not tied to the convoy.

Admiral Ingersoll simply told us to operate in the vicinity of the Azores against submarines. Those were the orders he gave you, which gave you plenty of elbow room to write your own ticket. So we were not tied to a convoy.

We would go out and hunt submarines as best we could. Of course, we relied very heavily on the daily broadcast from Washington from the Tenth Fleet - the estimate of the submarine situation in the Atlantic, which they put out every day. And they would pinpoint the location of all submarines that they'd had reports on in the past twenty-four hours. Then they would also estimate where other submarines were - that is, that they knew that a submarine had been at a certain point let us say three or four days ago. They would estimate where he was going, and where he was today, and where he would be the next day, and so on.

There was a Commander Ken Knowles in Washington who ran this submarine estimate thing. He was just a sooth sayer. He could put himself in the position of a German skipper and just figure out what that guy was going to do, and where he would go. He was absolutely uncanny in his predictions.

I treated this Cominch daily estimate as Bible truth every day, and we based our operations on it completely.

One reason why I did was that the very first thing that happened on this first cruise was we got a special message from Cominch from the Tenth Fleet saying, "There is going to be a refueling rendevouz of submarines off the Azores at a certain point at sunset on a certain day." It just gave us that information.

We were going to be reasonably close to it so I laid off about a hundred miles from that point until about four in the afternoon. Then we launched eight torpedo planes to search that area. And right at sunset we caught the refueler with a sub alongside, hoses stretched across, and another sub standing by waiting for his turn. We caught them and we blasted the hell out of the refueler and the guy alongside of him. We sank the refueler, an auxiliary tanker. The one that was taking fuel - we thought we got him too, but we found out after the war that he was able to limp back in to Brest.

Right after the attack we could see junk and oil and everything all over the ocean. There were about thirty survivors swimming around in the water.

After that experience, just following the Cominch estimate exactly, turning out the way it did, I believed everything that I heard from then on. That was our first cruise.

Q: Did the German subs in any way use any of the Azores, any of the Islands?

Gallery: No, they didn't use them. We were in the Azores by this time.

Q: But there are so many Islands there, and they are scattered.

Gallery: No, they would have their refuelers around the Azores, but they didn't actually use the Islands.

The night we made this kill, we made the kill right at sunset, it was about forty miles from the ship to the spot where the sub was sunk and I had eight planes in the air.

There were only three, I think, that were in on the

attack. The others were spread out, that was quite an area we were searching. But the others all heard the report of the attack. So each one of those other eight guys figured it was absolutely essential for the war effort for him to get over there and take a gander at these Germans swimming around in the water.

Here it was just about sunset, and up to this time nobody in the Atlantic had flown at night off the CVEs. The idea was you always got your plane back just before dark.

This was an overcast day and I knew it was going to be darker than hell that night, and here this kill was at sunset, so we had to get those guys back. I kept screaming at them to get the hell back to this ship and land.

But as I say, these guys all figured it was essential for the war effort to have a look at those guys in the water. So they flew over there and had a look. Eventually they got back to the ship, and when they got back it was damn near dark. The first three got aboard all right.

The fourth one went off the side of the flight deck and nosed down in the gallery walkway. So we had to get this guy out of there.

We were a brand new ship then. We just got butter fingered and clumsy that night, and we couldn't get that plane out of the gallery walkway. We tried everything we knew, we just couldn't budge it. I even tried to flip it over the side, by turning the ship real sharp and putting a list on it and then shoving it over, but we couldn't get rid of it.

Meantime, it was getting darker and darker all the time. Finally it was pitch black. We finally straightened up into the wind again, with this plane down in the side.

I called the guys in the air, there were four of them in the air then, and I made a pitch to them and said, "Now, look, the tail of that plane sticks out a little bit on the flightdeck, but not much. If you guys will land just the least little bit over to the port side of the ship, you won't hit the tail."

I got some very skeptical and reluctant 'rogers' back from the air. Then we started making passes and tried to bring those guys in.

We were lit up like a barroom on a Saturday night, because we had to. We lit everything up, but it was black. And the boys had not done any night flying. They were jittery and they made some of the wildest passes I have ever seen.

We had to keep waving them off, waving them off, waving them off. Meantime, they were burning up their gasoline.

So we finally in desperation gave one guy a 'cut,' and he came down, hit his wheels on deck, bounced in the air, rolled over on his back, and dove into the water.

Our plane guard destroyer picked up all three of the guys in the plane and saved them. But that was enough of that.

So I told the other three guys, "Now you land in the water. We'll have our destroyer turn the search lights on."

Q: The water was smooth around there?

Gallery: It was reasonable North Atlantic stuff.

"You land in the water and we'll pick you up," and they landed in the water, and we did pick them up. We got everybody back that night, but that was what turned the tide for me on this night flying. I decided that from then on we are going to learn to fly at night.

The first thing we did the next day, we took this 'turkey' that had gone into the gallery walkway. By that time we had it back on deck again.

For the rest of that cruise for the next two weeks every day, morning and afternoon, we would take that plane and roll it off the side of the deck into the gallery walkway, and the boys would drag it back on again. By the time they had done that about a dozen times, they were real experts at it and they could whip it out of there in a couple of minutes. And by the time we got back to Norfolk, they were damn sick and tired of it, too. So I finally let them give the thing a military funeral by shoving it over the stern end of the deck into the water. By that time it was pretty well battered, it wasn't worth overhauling.

Then when we got in from that cruise, we got a new squadron aboard for the next cruise. The first thing I did was to get the skipper in and tell him that this cruise we start flying at night.

I told him what I proposed to do was to start with a full moon. Then they would be flying each night with the moon getting a little smaller until eventually, in twelve days, there would be no moon. They'd be flying absolutely black. He went along with this idea. He said, "Okay, we'll have a shot at it."

This was a new squadron and they were new at the job. They had done some carrier landing practice ashore, but they hadn't done any at sea.

So on the next cruise we started off the first full moon that we had and started them flying at night. That was pretty hairy because what the hell, when you're breaking the ice on a brand new business, it's bound to be hairy.

On the first half of that cruise on the way from Norfolk to Casablanca, we flew all day long every day, bringing the last planes in just before sunset. And we never did get the kind of weather that I wanted to start the night flying, and the moon wasn't right anyway. So this was purely a daytime operation on the way to Casablanca. We flew all day long every day and never saw a damn thing.

Then on the way back things happened to break for us just right. The night of the full moon it was a nice calm sea. And so we started our night flying.

That very night we got the U-515. We caught him on the surface, charging his battery, and drove him down. Then we hounded him all night. Every time he'd pop up, we'd nail him again and chase him down again.

Making a depth charge attack on a sub at night, or even in the daytime, is not a hundred percent thing. You don't get the kill every time, and especially at night you don't.

But we would drive him down every time. We drove him down three or four times that night.

Then in the meantime we had broken off a couple of destroyers with my escort to get over there to that spot. They got there about seven o'clock in the morning, right over the spot where this guy was. Then from seven that morning until one that afternoon, these destroyers were working this guy over.

He was a hell of a sub skipper incidentally, Werner Hencke. He knew all the tricks of the trade. He was down at six hundred feet. He was squirming around and would do all sorts of tricks on us.

And we were dropping depth charges all over the ocean, but finally about two o'clock in the afternoon we shook him up bad enough so that he figured the gig was up. His battery was shot by that time anyway. So he finally surfaced right in the middle of the task group.

We blasted away at him then with everything that we had. He finally up ended and sank. We picked up forty-five out of the fifty-five people in his crew.

This was the very first night that we'd been flying at night. During that night we had made another contact, or thought we had made another contact, on another sub. So as soon as we got Hencke, we sent out a search for the second sub. And we got him the next night.

So here the first two nights we flew, we got two kills. We had gone three weeks before flying in the daytime with no kills at all. The thing being that the subs simply did not come up in the daytime, they came up at night. If you wanted to do business out there, you had to fly at night.

Q: They weren't on to that new technique either, were they?

Gallery: No, they weren't.

Of course when we got back from that cruise and reported this, then all the other CVEs started night flying. But we broke the ice on it.

There was one interesting sidelight to the sinking of the U-515. That was the one that was commanded by Oberlieutenant Werner Hencke, who was one of the U-boat aces. He had the Iron Cross with Oak Leaves. He was a very ambitious guy and he was out to get diamonds for his Iron Cross.

In fact, his crew blamed his overweening ambition to get diamonds for the loss of their ship. They said that if he hadn't been so damn set on getting diamonds, we wouldn't have got them, and that he would have gotten away.

When we got Hencke and his men aboard the Guadalcanal, we immediately separated them into three groups. We took all the non-rated men and we locked them up in one compartment, all the rated men in another compartment, and then we took the four officers and put them in the brig. We kept them separated as long as they were on the ship, so that they couldn't talk to each other and give each other pep talks on security.

The day after we got these people, Hencke sent word up from the brig that he wanted to see me. So I had him brought up to the cabin. He registered a protest about being kept in the brig. He quoted the

Geneva Convention to me and said that he was entitled to an officer's stateroom and to eat in the wardroom and so forth and so on.

I didn't have a copy of the Geneva Convention handy at the time, but I told him that this was completely impracticable on this ship. I said, "Among other things we've got a hell of a lot of crew members on this ship who are of Jewish extraction and a lot of Poles. These lads might not be very polite to you if I gave you the run of the ship. You'll just have to do the best you can in the brig." So he went back to the brig.

And then about three days later my Chief Master at Arms came up to me with this story - he had gotten acquainted with Hencke because he brought him his food, and talked to him while he was eating. Hencke told the Chief Master at Arms that just before the U-515 had sailed on that cruise, she was on her way out from Lorient when we got her, they had heard a broadcast from England - this was a propaganda broadcast beamed at the U-boat bases - in which the British said they had just learned that it was the U-515 which had sunk the Ceramic about a year before. (The Ceramic was a big passenger liner that ran to Australia.) And she was sunk with the loss of all hands, except one man, off the Azores about a year before with a very heavy loss of life, around 800 people. It seemed that after torpedoing the Ceramic, the sub that did this job had surfaced and picked up one soldier to bring back in as proof. All the rest of the people were lost, because it turned out there was a hell of a storm that came up right afterwards.

They got this one soldier back to Germany and they had him go on a broadcast and announce that he had been saved and that the Ceramic was sunk.

The British announced on their broadcast to the U-boat bases that they found it was the U-515 that sunk the Ceramic. And they said, "We have learned that the U-515 surfaced and machine gunned survivors in the lifeboats. If we ever get anybody from the U-515, we're going to try them as pirates."

Hencke denied this indignantly - the machine gunning of survivors. And I believed him, I don't think he did.

But anyway, this was what the British said. And this was the story that Hencke recited to my Chief Master at Arms. So the Chief Master at Arms came up and told me about it.

I meant to say - when Hencke had been protesting about my treatment of him, of putting him in the brig, I had said to him - this was just a shot in the dark - "If you don't like the way I'm treating you, we're going in to Gibraltar to refuel, I'll turn you over to the British." As I say, this was just a shot in the dark. We weren't going anywhere near Gibralter, but this was the story I told him. I didn't know about the British propaganda. And I said, "We could turn you over to the British." He said, "Well, no, no, it's not that bad, don't do that." So I said, "All right."

Anyway, when the Chief Master at Arms came up and told me this story, I began putting two and two together. I began to wonder how far can I push this thing of turning him over to the British.

So I drew up a sheet of official paper a statement saying, "I, Werner Hencke, Oberlieutenant German Navy, hereby promise on my honor that if I am imprisoned in the United States instead of in England, I'll answer all questions truthfully when interrogated." Then I had a place for him to sign, for me to sign, and my Exec to sign as witness.

I figured this is something where I've got nothing to lose and a possibility of gaining something. The only thing that could happen is Hencke could spit in my face, which won't affect the outcome of the war one way or the other. But if he falls for it, maybe something good will come of it.

So I had Hencke brought up to the cabin. On the desk I had the chart of Gibraltar laid out, with dividers and things on it as if I were looking over the anchorage of Gibraltar, because I told him that we were going in there. And he saw it.

Then I had a phony dispatch from Cominch, which I

gave to Hencke. The dispatch said, "The British have requested when you refuel in Gibraltar you turn over Hencke and his crew to them. In view of the crowded condition of your ship, you are authorized to use your discretion." This was from Cominch to me.

I handed this dispatch to Hencke. His face fell when he read it, and he said, "Well, I suppose there's nothing you can do about it." I said, "There is. This dispatch authorized me to use my discretion. If you make it worth my while, I'll take you to the United States." So he said, "What do you want me to do?" I said, "Just sign this," and shoved the paper across the table at him.

This was sort of like a scene from a movie you might say. He read the thing and said, "You know, of course, that I can't sign this." I said, "Well, it's up to you. If you sign it, you go to the United States. If you don't, you and your crew go to England."

So he thought that over for a minute or two. And then he picked up the pen and he signed it. So we sent Hencke back to the brig.

Then I had a photostat made of this thing Hencke had signed and passed that around among his whole crew. And I made a similar proposition to everyone in the crew, except specifying in much greater detail as to what they would talk about and asked them to sign it. So they all figured - what the hell, the skipper's talking, so why shouldn't we? Every one of them signed it.

Then when we got back into Norfolk, we turned these guys in, and I turned the papers in. ONI went to work on the thing.

Hencke of course reneged on his agreement, as I was sure he would, and said it was obtained under false pretenses and duress and so on. He didn't talk, he didn't say a word.

But his crew didn't know that. They'd had no communication with him. We'd kept them separated. They all figured - the skipper is singing, why shouldn't we? And they sang like a bunch of canary birds. ONI got plenty out of them.

Q: He was stupid to have spilled the beans in the first place, wasn't he, to have talked about this message that they picked up?

Gallery: Yes, it was stupid, sure. I don't know why he did.

Then the finale to this thing was rather tragic - Hencke eventually found out that the crew had been talking and it preyed on his mind.

Then ONI said to Hencke, "Either you talk or we're going to send you to England in accordance with your agreement."

Hencke still wouldn't talk. So they got ready to send him to England. He was in a prisoner of war camp. The day before he was supposed to leave, Hencke just walked over to the fence and started climbing it. The sentry hailed him and called at him to halt, and he didn't halt. So the sentry shot him and killed him.

Q: It's a way of committing suicide.

Gallery: Yes, actually he committed suicide.

So that was the U-515. The next day we got the U-68. These two incidentally were old time U-boats. Between the two of them they'd sunk around 350,000 tons. The U-68 was one of the real old timers.

We caught that one right at sunrise, the planes coming in out of the west, with the sun rising in the east. They were coming in out of the dark. So they caught them completely unaware on the surface with only three lookouts up on the conning tower when they hit.

Q: Your planes had been out on reconnaissance?

Gallery: Yes, they had been out all night hunting for him. They caught him just at sunrise.

We caught them on the surface with nothing but lookouts up in the conning tower. And we plastered them with machine guns, rockets, depth charges, and a homing torpedo. We broke them in two, so down he went and left the three lookouts swimming around in the water.

The planes that had made the kill dropped a lifecraft in the water for the men there, and they radioed us. We were about sixty miles away. Then we kept one plane over the spot circling, so we could see him on radar to guide us in.

About four hours later, we got over there and picked up the survivors. There were only two of them left by that time. One of them was dead, the other one was swimming around and holding his dead friend up. So there was just one survivor that we got, and he was near gone when we got him. His name was Kastrup.

The next day I got him up to the cabin, and he was still in pretty shaky condition. And I asked him a few questions, which he had no business answering.

I'll never forget this young kid. After I asked him his name and his rate and so on, and the name of his U-boat, which he answered, then I began asking some other questions about U-boats operations which he had no business answering. He just shook his head, he said, "No, he wouldn't answer that." I said, "Well, you should answer."

The angle I worked on him was this - I said, "Your skipper, when your sub was attacked, closed the hatch on you and the other lookouts and submerged, and left you up there to your own devices. In other words, he abandoned you. Therefore you should have no loyalty to him, you should talk."

I'll never forget this young guy. He looked me right in the eye and said, "Ich bin Deutsche Soldaten." (I'm a German soldier.) And he wouldn't say a damn word. And I've always had great respect for that guy.

This happened on Easter Sunday morning. I send him an Easter card each year, and I get an answer back from him. He's living now in Essen in Germany.

Q: You were able to quiz him in German?

Gallery: No, I had an interpreter there. But when he said, "Ich bin Deutsche Soldaten," I didn't need any interpreter for that.

That was the second cruise. The name of the skipper of that squadron was Dick Gould. I recommended that squadron, which was the outfit which broke the ice for night flying, for the Presidential Unit Citation. I never found out whether they got it or not. But anyway they opened up night flying, because from then on it became routine in the Atlantic.

Actually when I got out to the Pacific, which was nearly a year later, and got aboard one of the big carriers out there, I found that naval aviation in the Pacific was still a dawn to dusk operation, with the exception of two or three specially trained night fighter pilots that each one of the big carriers had. But all the rest of them, they got them back in before sunset. This was on the big carriers, which made the Guadalcanal look like a little spit kit in size.

Q: This failure to train night fighters was kind of a carry over from the thirties, wasn't it, when our Navy didn't go in for night training of any kind?

Gallery: That's right.

When I was a carrier pilot, the night flying that we did was maybe two nights a year when there was a full moon, we would make four carrier landings on one of the big carriers. And that was it. Incidentally, a full moon makes a big difference.

Gallery #3 - 93

Rear Admiral Daniel V. Gallery

U. S. Naval Institute

Annapolis, Maryland

June 14, 1974

By: John T. Mason, Jr.

Mr. Mason: Admiral, it's always a delight to see you.

Last time you gave me a fascinating story, part of your activities in anti-submarine warfare in the Atlantic during World War II. You told me about the capture of the crew of the U-515, you told me about sinking the U-68, but there are further events in this story, and I hope you'll unravel them today.

Admiral Gallery: Our next cruise began in May of '44.

I told about how we had broken the ice on night flying on a previous cruise. I got the skipper of our new squadron, (who was coming out with us on this third cruise) in and told him that we proposed to fly all night and he went along with it.

Then another idea that I had gotten from this previous cruise was a rather far fetched one - of towing a submarine home.

Q: This idea more or less was born when you were in Iceland.

Gallery: That's where it was born, I think I discussed that, yes. And it was still stuck in the back of my mind.

I was pretty familiar with the habits of submarines by this time, and I knew that when you got one cornered and hammered him with depth charges and punished him so much that he figured he was finished and going to sink, it was standard operational procedure for submarines to blow their tanks and come up and abandon ship, give the crew a chance to get overboard so they could be rescued, and open the scuttling valves and sink the sub.

I knew this was their standard procedure, which they always followed, and I figured that in the heat of battle it was quite possible that a sub skipper would figure that he had had it prematurely and that he would surface before he really had to and abandon ship and open the scuttling valves. If we could get aboard in time and close the scuttling valves we might be able to keep it afloat and tow it home.

Q: You were gambling on the human element then, weren't you?

Gallery: Yes, that's right, and it was a long gamble, but of course the prize would be well worth the gamble. Among other things we'd get the submarine codes, which was the main thing we'd be after.

At the departure conference for this cruise where I had all my submarine skippers together, I outlined this plan to the boys and told them that I wanted everybody to organize boarding parties and to keep a whale boat ready to lower. And that if we brought a sub up on this next cruise, instead of immediately throwing the works at him and trying to blast him out of the water and sink him, we would just shoot a lot of small stuff at him to keep him away from his guns, discouraging him from shooting torpedoes, and to expedite his abandon ship rule, so the skipper could get his people off of there and we could get our people aboard and try to close the scuttling valves.

The destroyers that I had with me on this cruise were the same ones that I had on this previous cruise when we brought up the U-515. We hammered away at her for ten or fifteen minutes before she sank. In fact, I was beinning to think we'd have to ram her. So this idea wasn't too farfetched to this particular group.

At the departure conference we always had a lot of outsiders from CinCLant, from Cominch, from the ASW experts, and so on, just sitting back and listening. When we were discussing the capture business I saw some of these people look at each other and make circular motions with their fingers like - this guy is nuts, but they didn't say anything.

So we agreed that if we brought a sub up on this cruise we would try to get aboard and capture him.

We shoved off and started our regular routine of round the clock night flying. It went fine, the boys took to it and could handle it.

After about a month we were off the Cape Verde Islands and we were beginning to run low on fuel and we were going to have to head for Casablanca. Then we picked up a broadcast from Cominch on a homebound U-boat coming back from the Gold Coast in Africa which was not too far away from us. So we started hunting for him. We were on his tail for about a week.

Q: Did you get subsequent reports from Cominch on this?

Gallery: We got a daily report from Cominch, but that was just an estimate of where they thought he was. Those estimates, as I reported in the previous tape, were uncannily accurate as we found out later.

We based our daily operations on his estimate, and a number of times we got close to this guy. We got indications of a submarine - the disappearing radar blips and noisy sonar buoys and things of that kind, which you can't be sure of, but later on we were sure of them. But he'd get away from us each time. This had gone on for about a week.

Finally we were getting low on fuel. Our Chief Engineer was up warning me that, "By God, we'd better get into Casablanca or we were going to run out of fuel." Knowing the Chief I knew that he always kept a little bit up his sleeve, so I kept pushing him and pushing him. Finally he said, "This is the last night we can possibly operate." We operated that last night, and got more indications but again got no contact.

So the next day, Sunday, we were heading for Casablanca. We gave up the hunt and headed for Casablanca. Along about noon on Sunday our destroyers ran right over this guy. He had made a detour in toward the coast during the night and was on his way back out again and we were right over him.

We caught him completely by surprise. He was running submerged and a destroyer picked him up on sonar. We depth charged him. The first attack shook him up a bit, but didn't do much damage.

Our planes in the air could see this guy in clear water. This isn't often you can do this, but they spotted him running submerged and they were able to coach our destroyers right over him.

We dropped another depth charge which shook him up pretty badly, rolled him over on end under water and dumped everybody into the bilges. They were just sitting down to their Sunday dinner and everything was dumped on top of them. They jammed his rudder hard over, and it created panic among the crew. The crew came swarming out of the after torpedo room yelling that the pressure hull had been ruptured, and that the after torpedo room was flooding. The skipper took their word for it.

So he blew his tanks and surfaced and abandoned ship. He came up and the crew went overboard and left the sub running at about seven knots on the surface with the rudder jammed hard over running in a big circle.

She popped up almost in the middle of the Task Group. The destroyers immediately opened up on them with their small stuff - twenty millimeter and machine guns and some three-inch - and the crew went overboard.

Meantime, we dropped our boats in the water. The boat from the Pillsbury was the first one to get there. Lieutenant David was in charge of the boarding party of ten men. They chased the sub around in the circle and finally caught up with it, and threw a line aboard. A boy jumped out of the whale boat and tied it to the back of the submarine.

When he did incidentally I was about half a mile away and watching this thing through the binoculars, of course. I broadcast over the loudspeaker, "Hi, ho Silver, ride 'em cowboy," when they got the line aboard.

Then David and two other lads, Anispul and Wdowiak, were the first aboard. They beat it up to the conning tower, which was open.

We'd seen a number of people go overboard, but we were by no means sure that everybody had gone overboard. It was a good chance that there were still people on board waiting for them down there to greet them with a machine gun.

But David, Anispul, and Wdowiak plunged down the conning tower and found to their amazement that the sub was all theirs. That is, it was all theirs if she didn't sink or blow up. She was completely abandoned, the skipper and everybody gone.

But she was in almost neutral buoyancy by this time, just about ready to up end and go down, and water was pouring into her. And as far as I knew there were booby traps all over her and so on.

They soon found the place where the water was coming in, which was the bilge strainer that had the cover knocked off. The water was pouring in through that. Then one of the boarding board found the cover which was lying right there on the floor plate, luckily for us. If the thing had gone down in the bilges where he couldn't find it we wouldn't have been able to save her. He was able to put that cover back in place and set up

Q: That must have been quite a feat with the pressure -

Gallery: It was a lot of pressure, but he had a lot of incentive, too, to get it back.

He got it in and screwed up on the nuts and stopped the water just in the nick of time. You can see in the movies that we got that day she was right on the verge of upending and going down when he got it.

Then the Pillsbury came up alongside her to try to take her in tow. Why the Pillsbury tried to take her in tow alongside I never found out. Instead of taking her in tow astern she tried to take her in tow alongside.

They have these big bow flippers that stick out in the water. The bow flippers cut into the side of the Pillsbury and ripped a long underwater gash in her and flooded the two main compartments. The Pillsbury had to back clear. Then for a while I thought we were going to lose her because she had flooded the two compartments.

The Pillsbury radioed to me that she didn't think a destroyer could do this towing job. So I said, "All right, destroyers stand clear, I'll take her in tow myself."

I took the Guadalcanal over and backed down and put the stern up close to her bow and got a tow line over. By that time we had maybe twenty of our people on board the sub.

While I was lying there with the bow of this sub not more than twenty feet from my stern I said sort of a short prayer. I said, "Dear Lord, I've got some young lads on board that submarine. Please don't let any of them monkey with the firing switch or torpedoes."

Well, they didn't, and we finally got her in tow and started to haul her away. It soon developed that she sheared way out to starboard until the tow line was as taut as a bow string, but anyway, we were able to drag her along because the rudder was jammed. We were able to tow her all that afternoon.

Q: Didn't this entail a great demand on what fuel you had left?

Gallery: By this time I was in a spot where I couldn't get to Casablanca, I didn't have enough fuel left. I sent a message then to CinCLant saying we had boarded and captured this sub and that I didn't have enough fuel to get to Casablanca and requested permission to take her into Dakar.

I got an answer back from CinCLant almost immediately saying, "Nothing doing on Dakar. Take her to Bermuda," which was 2500 miles away. "We'll have a tanker rendezvous with you with fuel." So that got me off the spot with the fuel.

Q: Why did they turn down Dakar?

Gallery: Dakar was infested with German spies. If we had taken her into Dakar the Germans would have known about it immediately. So we should take her to Bermuda, and this got me off the spot on the fuel.

That almost won a place in naval history comparable to the Polish virgins by running out of oil, which would be very damn embarrassing - having to get towed in.

But when I sent my request for a tanker in with a P.S. on the end of it, "I've got a captured sub in tow," it was all right then. So that got me off the hook on that.

Here's one little interesting sideline on this thing. We had a custom on my ship of having the Padre say a morning prayer every morning on the loudspeaker.

When we were getting ready to put this ship in commission, I had been reading the reports of the battles out in the Pacific and in several of them I noticed that the skipper of the ship told about having the Padre get on the loudspeaker just before the battle started and say a prayer.

I discussed this with my Chaplain, Father Welden, who is now the Bishop of Springfield, and we both agreed that this would be bad psychology as well as rather shabby theology to wait until you're looking down the enemy's gun barrels before you ask God for help. So instead of that we'd said, "We'll do it every day as a matter of ships routine," so we did.

Every morning the Padre would get out the colors, and the boatswain's mate would ask for attention to the morning prayer. Everybody would stop what they were doing and face the colors and the Padre would say a short non-sectarian prayer to which everybody could say, "Amen."

Incidentally, I hope the Supreme Court doesn't hear about this because if they do they may declare everything we ever did on that ship unconstitutional and make us give that sub back to the Germans.

That evening just at sunset I was up on the bridge looking aft at this thing we had in tow, still hardly believing it. Father Welden came up to the bridge. I said to him, "Well, Padre, it looks like your morning prayer worked this morning." He said, "Yes, Captain, it sure does."

Then he told me this story about the Bishop of Dublin. He said, "The Bishop of Dublin was driving down the road one Sunday morning and he came across one of his flock who had a flat tire, and was pulled off on the side of the road trying to change it. The flat tire was stuck on the rim and Pat couldn't budge it no matter how hard he heaved. He was painting the air blue with a lot of bad language while he was trying.

So the Bishop stopped and took him to task for his bad language. He said, "Now Pat instead of cursing and swearing like that you ought to try prayer." So Pat said, "Yes, your worship, let's do that." So the two of them bowed their heads and said a short prayer.

Then Pat spit on his hands and got ready to heave again and just the instant he touched the tire it popped right off in his hands, whereupon the Bishop said, "Well, I be God damned."

Father Welden said, "I feel exactly the same way when I look aft at that thing we've got in tow."

Q: Were you in communication with your boarding crew all the time? You were directing them as to what they could do to facilitate things?

Gallery: By this time we had everybody back on board because we were afraid the thing was going to sink. We weren't sure if we were going to keep her, whether she'd stay afloat or not. So I didn't leave anybody on board during the night, we brought them back on our ship.

As soon as the sun went down all of our lookouts and our sonar operators and radar operators let their imagination run away with them, because everybody was all worked up with the excitement of the afternoon.

The minute the sun went down everybody began seeing hobgoblins all around us. The sonar people were getting firm echoes, the radar people were getting disappearing radar blips, and the lookouts were sighting periscopes. It sounded like we were completely surrounded by the German U-boats and they were closing in on us.

So I towed the thing a little bit too fast and busted the tow line. Then we had to circle it the rest of the night.

The first thing in the morning we got out a bigger tow line and got that aboard. While we were getting it aboard I went over to the thing myself to try to get the rudder amidships because the boys had reported to me that the rudder was jammed, and they couldn't move it with the electric steering gear, and the door to the after torpedo room was closed, which was where the hand steering was, and they said it had a booby trap on it.

At the departure conference I had told the boys, "In case we encounter any booby traps that's my pigeon. I'll take care of that," because I was an ordnance P.G. and I knew something about fuses and that kind of stuff. I was just itching for an excuse to get over there myself anyway.

So I went over and we went back to the after torpedo room and the water right door was closed. The main panel on the door had an open cover of a fuse box lying across it so that you couldn't open the door without closing the cover to this fuse box. This was what the boys thought was a booby trap, because there were a lot of electrical connections in the fuse box. They thought, "Maybe if we close this thing it will set something off."

I looked it over and I decided that it was not a booby trap. So I closed the cover to the fuse box. One of the nice things about that sort of business is that you find out right away whether you were right or not. And I was right, nothing happened.

Then we opened the door to the after torpedo room. We had to do that very carefully because according to the Germans it was flooded, and we didn't want to flood the rest of the boat. So we had to crack it very carefully and make sure that no water came out. And it didn't, it was dry. We got back in there and got at the hand steering gear and connected it up and brought the rudder back amidships.

Incidentally, while we were back there it occurred to me that here we were on a U-boat which was down by the stern about fifteen degrees and almost neutral buoyancy ready to up end any minute. I remember that one of the ways that submariners have of trimming their ship is to send a number of people all the way forward or all the way aft. Here we were, four of us, all aft on this thing which was down by the stern fifteen degrees.

Again we got away with it, but as soon as we got the rudder amidships I said, "Let's get the hell out of here," which we did.

Q: I suppose Admiral, common sense was on your side in terms of 'booby trap or no booby trap'; taken by surprise like that they didn't have time to do anything, did they?

Gallery: This was one of the main things I was relying on. They figured it was going to be on the bottom in another couple of minutes, so they didn't set any booby trap. Not only that, but they had thirteen five-pound demolition charges set along in the keel, and they had a switch up in the conning tower which could be set on anything from a few seconds to three or four minutes. When they left the ship they could set that thing so that after whatever time it was set it would blow up and that would be the end of it.

Q: Was that a uniform kind of installation?

Gallery: Yes, and we knew about this ahead of time. We knew that they had that sort of installation. So the first thing we did when we got aboard - we didn't know where the switch was or how it worked, but we would run along and look down in the bilges and we could see these fifty-pound charges. We'd reach down and get hold of the wires and yank them off. In the first few minutes on board we found twelve of these things but we knew there was one more. We didn't find that for two weeks.

In the meantime, a day or so later, we found the switch that operated them and we found that it was left unset. It wasn't set to fire anything.

The thing was that the Germans were so sure that when they abandoned ship that she was going to be on the bottom in another couple of minutes that they just neglected to set the firing.

Q: Was she easier to tow after you had gotten in there and righted the rudder?

Gallery: Yes, she towed very neatly from the stern and everything was fine.

I towed her for three days I believe. We were right in the middle of a submarine operating area at the time, so I figured we had to protect ourselves. We had to keep our planes in the air, so we resumed flight operations with this thing in tow.

At times I couldn't tow more than eight knots, that was as fast as I dared to go. And at times we only had ten knots of wind across the deck. You had to have twenty-five knots to fly off one of those baby flattops, but we did it anyway, and the boys were able to handle it. It goes to show that when the chips are down the boys rise to the occasion.

Q: What about the fueling problem?

Gallery: Three days after we got her in tow we rendezvoused with a tanker. She came alongside and filled us up and filled our destroyers up. Then we proceeded to Bermuda towing this thing.

We had one destroyer that could make three or four more knots than any of the rest of us. Among the things that we got off the sub were the operations code books and their cipher. We put them in a sack and put them in this other destroyer and sent her on ahead of us. She rushed this thing to Bermuda where it was picked up air and flown to Washington.

They immediately put a watch on U-boat frequencies and for the rest of the war we read their traffic of U-boats. Of course, the Germans had periodic changes that they made about every two weeks in the code, but the key to all the changes they made were in the code books that we captured, so we could follow the changes right along. We read their stuff for the rest of the war.

Q: When did they learn of the fate of this sub?

Gallery: They learned at the end of the war that we had captured this U-boat.

That leads me to what I think was probably the most remarkable part of this whole remarkable episode - that is the fact that we were able to keep it secret, which was very important on account of the code books. If they had known they were captured they would have thrown away the old code books and put in completely new code books, and we wouldn't have been able to read their stuff. So it was very important to keep the capture a secret.

But when we were towing this thing to Bermuda here I had 2500 young lads in my Task Group, all of them just bursting with the best story of their lives. I had to get them together and explain to them the vital necessity of keeping their mouths shut. They couldn't say a word to anybody when they got home, not even their wives, mothers, sweethearts, nobody. That's one hell of a big order.

I'm proud indeed of the fact that the boys did keep their mouths shut and the Germans didn't find out about this capture until the war was over. I think that speaks very highly indeed of devotion to duty and sense of duty and sense of responsibility of the average young American in bell bottom trousers.

Q: Whose background didn't necessarily include the security measures.

Gallery: That's right, yes.

We towed her into Bermuda and we left her in Bermuda. When we arrived in Bermuda, of course, there was a large delegation of experts from the Navy Department there to take over and inspect it and all the rest of it. She was kept in Bermuda for the rest of the war, and her crew were all interned in Bermuda in a special camp all by themselves.

The idea of leaving her in Bermuda was that Bermuda was an island and the British had very tight control over everything going out by mail, telephone, radio, press. And they were able to clamp an ironclad lid on the thing so word couldn't get out. If we'd brought her into Norfolk or any place in the United States, of course, it would have been out in no time, but they were able to keep it secret. Then the fact that the crew were kept separate from any other German prisoners - there wasn't any word getting back that way through mail.

Q: Incidentally, how did the crew react to the fact that the submarine didn't sink and that you had her?

Gallery: They took a dim view of it, they didn't like it.

Incidentally, we shot the skipper in the leg with a fifty caliber and he eventually lost that leg. When we got him aboard my ship he was down at sick bay and he hadn't actually seen us take his sub in tow.

I went down to see him in sick bay the next day and told him that we had his sub in tow, and he didn't believe it. So I sent over to his cabin and got a picture of his wife and kids off the desk and gave it to him, then he believed it. Then he kept shaking his head and saying, "I will be punished for this, I will be punished for this."

I tried to reassure him that they already had lost the war, that Hitler and his mob would be thrown out at the end of the war, and that they'd forget about it, but he wouldn't believe it. He kept shaking his head and saying, "I will be punished for this."

And as a matter of fact when the war was over in a way he was punished for a while, because the Germans have a very elite society now composed of survivors of the U-boat fleet with headquarters in Hamburg. Only about twenty percent of the active U-boat fleet survived the war. They had eighty percent casualties, which is a terrific casualty rate. So there's this very elite society of former U-boat sailors and Lange, the skipper of the U-505, was barred from membership of this society on account of the capture.

When I heard about this I wrote to Krutchmer, who was the number one ace of aces and the head man in the U-boat survivors fraternity. I wrote to him and said I thought it was unfair to bar Lange from membership because he was simply the victim of circumstances - he had done everything that he should have done, and he had done the same thing that 780 other guys had done, but nobody had ever tried to board them before.

And I apointed out to Krutchmer in my letter, I said, "The same thing could have happened to you, Krutchmer," because he was captured by the British. A British destroyer had laid alongside his sub for fifteen minutes and then the sub went down. They could have gotten aboard then and taken his sub.

I had a nice letter back from Krutchmer thanking me for my letter and saying that he agreed with me and that they had lifted the suspension on Lange. And he was allowed to join the fraternity.

Eventually I got to be good friends with Lange. I looked him up about seven or eight years after the war when I was in Germany. I was in Hamburg and I looked him up. I wasn't sure that he'd be glad to see me because I hadn't been too polite to him that day we first met, but he was. He took the whole day off from his business and showed me all around Hamburg. He took me to lunch at his club, to dinner at his home, and to the theater afterwards.

That's a funny way to make friends with a guy - you shoot his leg off and take his ship away from him, but we got to be good friends.

Q: There was an aftermath to that story, too, in terms of the submarine itself.

Gallery: Yes, the sub itself is now at the Museum of Science and Industry in Chicago. Before I get into that there's one thing that I want to cover in connection with the capture.

We found out later that the U-505 had started off about two years before as quite a successful U-boat. On her first couple of cruises she sank 45,000 tons, five or six ships, and she got off to a good start with her first skipper.

Then she got a new skipper and he just had bad luck. He brought her over here to the Caribbean and she got bombed by a plane out of Trinidad. The bomb hit the U-boat and did a lot of damage to it, but didn't sink it. Incidentally, the bomb blew up the plane that dropped it, he dropped it so low that he blew himself up, and he was lost.

The sub was able to limp back to Lorient, on the surface all the way. Then it spent practically all the next year being repaired in Lorient. She was subjected to a lot of sabotage by French workers. They'd get her repaired and say, "Now you're all set to go out to sea and fire up." So they'd go to sea and something would go wrong - either somebody put sugar in the lube oil, or things of that kind.

One thing after another happened. Seven times the U-505 left Lorient presumably to go off on another operational cruise, and after a day or two had to come limping back in to have something else fixed.

This was at a time when we were really slaughtering the U-boats. A lot of U-boats were going out and never coming back, but the U-505 always came back. It began to get on the skipper's nerves. He began to imagine that people were looking at him kind of funny - this guy always comes back, there's something wrong with him.

So on the seventh cruise he told himself, "By golly, I'm not going to come back again." Some time out they were caught by a British destroyer in the Bay of Biscay. While he was down at 300 feet and trying to evade the destroyer, depth charges shook him up real badly, and this hard luck skipper hauled out his lugar and blew his brains out with his whole crew looking on.

Then his number two stepped into his shoes and took over and managed to elude the British destroyer. Then they surfaced and buried the skipper, and went back in to Lorient again.

The Germans should have broken up that crew and spread them around to a lot of different U-boats. Instead of that they kept them together, and put a new skipper in. That was Lange. Lange had to take over this demoralized crew and try to make something of them.

The next time they were attacked after their skipper had blown his brains out was when we attacked them, and they panicked.

We got any number of tremendously lucky breaks on this thing. Of course, you have to get the breaks to do a job, and we got them.

Q: Incidentally Admiral, did we learn anything in terms of ordnance from the captured sub?

Gallery: Yes. Technically we got the works - their torpedoes, their firing devices, their sonar, their radar, and of course their engines and all the rest of it. In addition we got all the standard operating instructions for submarines that were issued by Donitz. It was just a windfall of intelligence.

Q: Tell me about her eventual berth in Chicago.

Gallery: When Germany surrendered they brought the U-boat from Bermuda to the States, and they went on a war bond selling trip up and down the East Coast of the United States.

Then they put her in the Portsmouth Navy Yard, Portsmouth, New Hampshire, and just tied her up and left her there. She sat there for pretty near ten years with nobody on board, no maintenance, nobody taking care of her. Several times during that ten year period the Navy got ready to take her out and sink her. But each time they did I would put in a squawk and say, "I went to a lot of trouble to keep that thing afloat and I don't want it sunk."

Q: How did you learn about this?

Gallery: I kept my ears to the ground, and I found out about it. And I knew that there was a movement afoot in Chicago to bring her there, and that eventually maybe something would come of it. So I blocked several attempts to sink it.

Then I was assigned to duty in Chicago as Commander Naval Air Reserve Training with headquarters at Glenview, right there in Chicago.

When I got out there the Navy League got interested in bringing the thing in Chicago. Colonel McCormick of the <u>Tribune</u> and all the newspapers

We got a Mayor's committee to handle the thing.

The Navy was sort of cool to the idea, but said we could have it if we wanted it, if we could get it to Chicago. They weren't going to help us.

So we had to raise money to tow the thing from Portsmouth, New Hampshire to Chicago. They had to get a bill through Congress authorizing the transfer to the Museum of Science and Industry. The Museum had to agree in writing that in case of war if this thing was ever needed again the United States could have it back, and this sort of thing.

They got this committee together and raised around $300,000. And we towed it from Portsmouth, New Hampshire up the St. Lawrence River through the old St. Lawrence Seaway - this was before the new Seaway - to Chicago.

Incidentally, it just barely fit through the locks in the old Seaway. The sub was, as I remember, 253 feet long and the locks were 252 feet 11 inches long. So it was about an inch or two too long to go through the locks. But if you put it in the locks and then cocked it — if you put the bow in one corner of the locks and the stern in the other you could just barely get the locks closed. We got her in that way.

Q: That was fortunate. It would have been quite a portage if —

Gallery: We had another idea of bringing it up the Mississippi if we had to, because a lot of subs had been taken down the Mississippi during the war that were built in Milwaukee. But that was quite a job too, because you had to put them on a barge to get through the Canal.

Anyway, we finally got it to Chicago. We borrowed a floating drydock from the Great Lakes Dredging and Dock Company. We put her in the floating drydock, then we dredged a channel in to the beach at the Museum of Science and Industry.

The Museum incidentally is right at the beach. The Outer Drive at Michigan Avenue is between the Museum and the beach, that's all.

So we got her in to the beach. That's about five miles south of the Navy pier. Then we dragged it across Michigan Avenue one night.

Incidentally, my uncle, George Donahue, was the head of the South Park Board in Chicago and Michigan Avenue belonged to him. So I had to get permission from

Uncle George to drag this sub across his driveway.

The night we drug it across was the night of the Pro-College Football game up in Soldiers Field. So there was a tremendous amount of traffic up and down the drive that night, and we had to wait. The traffic at the start of the game had gone north. Then we drug it across. The traffic coming away from the game was detoured. We had until four o'clock the next morning to get it across, and then the drive had to be opened again.

That night I kept a jet airplane warmed up at Glenview. In case something broke down in the middle of the drive that night I was going to be long gone the next morning. I wasn't going to face Uncle George.

But we got it across in good time, and the drive was open for traffic the next morning.

Then we hauled it up alongside the Museum, and mounted it on concrete cradles. Incidentally, our chief engineer for this job - getting it out of the water, across the drive, and alongside the Museum - was Seth Gooder. He did a tremendous job for us. He built a special concrete cradle for it with rollers on it to allow for the expansion and contraction of the sub - in other words the heat and the cold of the winter.

About a month after we got it there we had the dedication ceremony, at which Admiral Halsey was the principle dignitary. Arthur Godfrey was the master of ceremonies. We had all of the original boarding party there on the reviewing stand. They had a big dinner in the Museum the night before at which the Secretary of the Navy, Thomas, attended and presented the Navy Commendation Ribbon to five of the main people that brought the sub to Chicago. So that was that.

Q: Admiral, tell me a little bit about the final cruise you had on the Guadalcanal in the Atlantic. After this episode with the U-boat the morale must have been high indeed.

Gallery: We were the cockiest bunch of so and sos that ever sailed the seas.

Of course, we got a new squadron, and we broke them in on the night flying the same as the others.

Q: Had they now been getting preliminary training in night flying at this stage?

Gallery: They were getting some ashore, yes, and they were beginning to get some in the Chesapeake, too. By now it was beginning to be understood that you could fly at night. So this outfit stepped right in and flew at night.

But the fourth cruise which we made was a dud, we

got nothing on that cruise. Early in the cruise we did one night catch a submarine on the surface with our planes. The planes made an attack on him, but didn't hurt him too much, drove him down. He was only about a hundred miles from where I was when they got him, so I figured this was another sure kill, because here we had a confirmed contact with him a hundred miles from us.

We spent the next month hunting that guy. He was on his way home, as we knew from the Cominch estimates. We had a pretty good idea as to how far he could go every day, and we had a Cominch estimate every day on where he was. We just camped on top of that guy for a month, flying around the clock, but never saw him again. I'd still like to know to this day where the hell that guy went, but we never saw hide nor hair of him.

Q: Did you attempt to find out from the log in Germany later on after the war?

Gallery: No, I never did, because I had very few clues to go on. I didn't even know his number. I would have had to start from the date, and it would have been quite a job to find out. But I'd still like to know where the hell that guy went, he got away from us.

Q: What area of the Atlantic was this in?

Gallery: This was just south of Bermuda. He was on his way home, and we trailed him almost all the way across the Atlantic, but we never got him.

Right after that I was detached from the Guadalcanal and went to duty in the Navy Department in the office of DCNO Air, in the planning section. I spent the next seven or eight months there.

Q: What were your actual duties in the planning section of BuAir?

Gallery: They were concerned with the logistics of the fleet - supplying the number of airplanes that they needed, and supplying the training, and supplying the pilots that they needed, and that sort of thing.

Q: All of that system was working pretty smoothly at that stage of the war.

Gallery: Yes, it was, it was really working very smoothly.

At that time a shore duty in the Navy Department was supposed to be at least a year, maybe a year and a half, but I had a pretty good drag with Uncle Ernie King by this time.

Incidentally, when we brought the U-505 home I had found in the skipper's cabin a big thick book in German. I forget what the name of it was, I think it was <u>Roosevelt's Kampf</u>, or something like that. This book was all about how President Roosevelt was out to dominate the world, and he was the villian of the book. I took this book and wrote something in the front of it to indicate where it had come from.

When I reported to Washington Admiral King had me in to lunch with him, and I gave him this book and suggested to him that he give it to the President, which he did.

Then the President wrote me a very nice letter thanking me for the book and saying it was being sent to the Library at Hyde Park. He sent the letter through official channels, but he sent it as a plain unclassified letter. Of course the capture, at this time, of the U-505 was super duper top secret. When the letter went through Admiral Lowe's shop they immediately picked up the breach of security. Admiral Lowe blew his top. He said, "God damn this guy Gallery is really spilling this." He sent for me and was about to flay my hide off for breaking security. After he got through with blasting me I said, "Oh sir, I didn't do this, Admiral King did it." That took the heat off me right away. But anyway I stood pretty well with Admiral King from that time on.

I was able to get out of the Navy Department after seven or eight months.

Q: Are there any meetings with King in that period, any episodes that you can recall, that might be of interest as they pertain to him?

Gallery: I'd see him now and then, but just to say good morning to, I actually had no contacts with him, just that lunch.

Q: At that lunch he wanted to get all the details of the story?

Gallery: Oh yes.
Then I went out to the Pacific to take command of the Hancock. I got there just before the surrender. Of course, ever since then my story is that the Japs surrendered for three reasons. One was the atomic bomb, two was Russia's entry into the war, and three was Gallery's arrival at Third Fleet. Anyway, they surrendered right after I got there.

Q: You were present then in Tokyo Bay. Can you tell me about that?

Gallery: Actually the day of the surrender I was flying over the Missouri. I went out with the air group that day and we flew over the Missouri at the time of the surrender.

Q: As part of that great armada of planes.

Gallery: Yes, it was a hair raising trip too, it was really something.

Q: There were so many planes.

Where were they landing, all over Japan, and carriers as well?

Gallery: No, on the carriers themselves. We were not in Tokyo Bay at that time, we were lying off shore a ways. The Missouri was in Tokyo Bay and one or two other ships, but most of the Fleet was still off shore.

Then I went down to Okinawa and picked up a load of soldiers and brought them back to the United States.

Then we made a trip from the United States to Manus and picked up another load of soldiers, and brought them back to the United States.

Q: They were from MacArthur's army?

Gallery: Yes, that's right.

After our second trip from Manus back to the United States I was promoted to Rear Admiral, and I was then transferred from the Hancock to command of a big carrier division at San Diego.

At that time the ships were tied up to the dock with only skeleton crew aboard, so for the next year we had darn little to do. In fact, I refer to that period of time as - operation stagnate.

Q: That's a very painful experience, isn't it, to have your crews evaporate underneath you? There's nothing you can do about it.

Gallery: Yes. Not a thing.

Q: Have you got some comments to make on that phenomenon that happens after every war?

Gallery: Just the obvious one - that apparently from now on there'll be nothing but peace and we didn't need a Navy any more. We found out before long this just wasn't so.

Of course, at that time we were the number one military power of the world, and there's no reason why we shouldn't have stayed so, but we didn't.

Q: What were your own personal feelings - achieving

flag rank at a time when the Navy was disintegrating?

Gallery: Of course, I was very much pleased to make flag rank. We still had quite a Navy left.

After about a year in this little carrier division I was brought to Washington and got a real good job there. I was made the Assistant CNO for guided missiles. I was the first one to have that job. As a matter of fact, I relieved Spike Blandy, who had that among a number of other jobs.

At that time there was a lot of talk about push-button warfare being just around the corner. A lot of things that are happening now, just twenty years later, were just a gleam in a few far seeing eyes then. I was right in on the beginning of a lot of that stuff.

Q: What was the status of missiles at that point? What did we have, what did we project?

Gallery: At that time all we had really was the ideas of a few far seeing people that had to be developed from scratch.

Q: Did these ideas stem from the experiments of Dr. Goddard largely?

Gallery: Goddard with his rockets was certainly one of the main people. He provided the propulsion. The guidance was something else.

When I got to Washington it was just about the time of the big unification uproar. Things were in quite a turmoil with all the talk about changing the whole set up of the Defense and the Army and the Navy to the Defense Department and splitting the Air Force off from the Army, and so forth and so on. There was a hell of an uproar.

One of the big moves of contention was what was going to happen to naval aviation, because the Air Force were out to take over naval aviation and the Navy didn't want them to do it. So that got to be quite a battle.

This was the time of the so-called revolt of the Admirals, and I was right in the middle of that.

Q: You've got to tell me that in detail.

Gallery: I was right in the middle of that battle, and was making speeches defending the Navy's position and getting in a bit of hot water on account of it.

This was about the time that I started writing in earnest. I wrote several articles for the <u>Saturday Evening Post</u> on the subject of unification. I got my tail in quite a crack with Louis Johnson, who was then the Secretary of Defense, because Louis disapproved of these articles and tried to stop them.

Q: How - with the editor of the Saturday Evening Post?

Gallery: He issued several directives which were addressed to the Secretaries of the Army and the Navy about what people could write about. As I say they were addressed to the Secretaries, they weren't addressed to me. So I governed my writings by the Navy regulations.

At that time the Navy regulations said that a naval officer could write about professional subjects and say anything they wanted provided they did not reveal any confidential information and provided they did not reveal any information which could be used against the United States in a law suit and one or two other things like that.

That was the only proviso in it, except that once an article was accepted for publication you then had to submit a copy of it to the Secretary of the Navy for his information. By the time that article was accepted for publication you had sold it to the Saturday Evening Post and you no longer had any control over it. This was the procedure that I followed with these articles.

Q: How many articles were there?

Gallery: One was entitled, "The Admiral Talks Back to the Airmen" - defending the Navy's right to keep it's own airplanes. Then another one, a follow up on that, was "Don't Let Them Sink the Navy."

Both of those by the time the copy according to the regulations got to the Secretary of the Navy and he had passed them to Louis Johnson, it was too late to stop them.

Louis Johnson at one time went up to Philadelphia to see the Saturday Evening Post and tell them, "You can't print that article." That was a very silly thing for Johnson to do because the folks just laughed at him and said they were going to print it anyway.

Q: Had SecNav actually tried to implement Johnson's directive?

Gallery: No, he hadn't. This was my out on the thing - that I was following the Navy regulations.

Q: The regulations that had existed for a long time.

Gallery: Yes. I had two articles in the Saturday Evening Post, both of which caused quite a flurry with Johnson.

Q: What sort of reaction from the public at large?

Gallery: A lot of interest, and I would say half the people apparently agreed with me and half didn't.

Then Louis Denfeld was the Chief of Naval Operations. He made an appearance before the Senate in which he took a very definite stand in the unification which antagonized the Secretary of the Navy and the Secretary of the Navy fired him.

I was out of Washington by then. I then wrote an article entitled, "If This Be Treason," which was published in Colliers. This was regarded by the new Secretary of the Navy, Mr. Matthews, his answer to the title of the article was, "Yes, this is treason."

When he got my advance copy he wrote me a letter, this was just before the article appeared in Colliers, saying, "This is treason, and the publication of this article will be considered conduct to the prejudice of good order and discipline," which is laying the foundation for a court martial. That gave me something to think about.

While I was still thinking and stewing about it I got this letter from the Secretary of the Navy's office. I figured when I opened it, "This is it, here's the specification for the court martial." But instead of that it was a very nice letter from Uncle Ernie King, patting me on the back for the article and saying he agreed with every word of it.

I now have those two letters framed and hanging on the bulkhead of my den at home.

Q: He had retired by that time.

Gallery: King never retired, five-star Admirals don't. That's why he was in the Secretary of the Navy's office, and that's why SecNav appears in the corner of the envelope.

Q: So he more or less cancelled out Matthews attitude.

Gallery: He didn't really cancel it out, he merely expressed his personal opinion on it.
   What happened was - Matthews got me in a little later and said this was something which he thought should be handled by the military end of the Navy rather than the civilian end, and so he was going to turn it over to Admiral Forrest Sherman, who by that time was CNO. Sherman referred it to me for a statement and I made a statement about it.
   The upshot of it all was that eventually instead of getting a general court martial, I got a letter of admonition from Forrest Sherman.
   After you've been threatened with a court martial and you wind up with a letter of admonition, I looked up

'admonition' in the dictionary. It's defined as a friendly advice.

I figured it was the equivalent of a letter of commendation. So that was that.

Q: Would you lap back and tell me about the job as missile deputy?

Gallery: We were just starting in the missile business then. A lot of people had ideas which have since grown into realities.

Q: What were they, what were some of these ideas that did come to be?

Gallery: At that time one of our main projects was the so-called 'bumblebee project' which was an anti-aircraft rocket. It ran jet propelled, guided by radar, which was a complete Buck Rogers at that time. It was undertaken by a Johns Hopkins group headed by Harry Hoffstad.

The name 'bumblebee' came from the fact that according to all the aerodynamic experts it's absolutely impossible for a bumblebee to fly, but the bumblebee just hadn't got the word about it and he flys anyway.

The 'bumblebee project' was regarded as more or less the same sort of thing. All the experts said it can't be done, but Larry Hoffstad and his people said they would do it anyway, and they did.

That has since developed into some of the anti-aircraft missiles that we have in the fleet now.

And at that time we were beginning to talk about pointing things into orbit around the earth. I remember we had an estimate on a moon rocket by the Martin Company. This was just to be an unmanned rocket, a rocket that would get to the moon, which never got anywhere. At any rate it indicated the lines along which we were thinking at the time.

We were setting up the Proving Grounds down at Cape Canaveral at that time. I was one of the people on the Joint Army-Navy-Air Force Committee that selected the site and set it up.

Q: What other sites did you consider?

Gallery: I've forgotten now. There was Point Mugu out on the West Coast, which later became the Navy launching point, and White Sands, which was the Army Proving Grounds.

Incidentally, at that time one of the things I promoted was the firing of a V-2 rocket off the <u>Midway</u>. We got a number of V-2 rockets from Germany, the rockets that they fired on London. We got a number of those rockets, they were down at White Sands. I got a number of these rockets and after a considerable hassle got permission to fire them off the <u>Midway</u>.

Q: What was your objective? What did you hope to learn?

Gallery: The main thing was at that time to focus high level attention in the Navy on the importance of this whole field, the missiles.

Q: Kind of a P.R. job?

Gallery: Yes, actually that's all if was really because we were never going to shoot rockets like the V-2 off the <u>Midway</u>. But I figured if we took one out on the <u>Midway</u> and fired it, it would attract a lot of attention and get a lot of people interested in rockets and in taking them to sea, which it did.

When we fired it off the <u>Midway</u> we had all the high brass in the Navy up there on the bridge of the <u>Midway</u> watching this thing. I'll never forget when the thing took off. It went up about twenty feet, it was supposed to go straight up to 20,000 feet, and then it leaned over about thirty degrees and went right smack over the bridge. I have never seen so many high ranking officers tramping all over each other to get out of the way when that happened. It went up to about 15,000 feet and broke itself apart, and that was that.

As a result of this thing - it accomplished its purpose, it focused a lot of attention on rockets and on guided missiles.

The first thing we got was the assignment of the Norton Sound as a missile ship. This was a brand new development in the Navy.

As a result of it they said, "We can't afford to risk something like the Midway shooting these silly rockets, but we will give you a special ship, the Norton Sound."

We got the Norton Sound as a result of this. She was a Navy ship of some kind. I think it was a destroyer tender or something of that kind. At any rate they made a lot of modifications in her and fitted her to launch rockets, and put in a lot of tracking gear and electronics and so on. So the Norton Sound played quite a part in the development of missiles.

Q: In selecting Cape Canaveral as the base for missile experiments and so forth, what were your requirements?

Gallery: For one thing you wanted a long over water range, which we had on the southeast. You didn't want it completely over uninhabited ocean, because you wanted to set up tracking stations along the way for radar to follow these missiles which we had through the islands of the Caribbean and various other islands in the South Atlantic. That was the main thing.

Q: It was an adequate kind of a runway that you had to have.

Gallery: Yes. Out in the Pacific at Mugu we didn't have any outlying islands. The closest ones were the Hawaiian Islands, a long ways away, but in the Atlantic we had these Caribbean Islands.

Q: In your period there then this selection was implemented with the actual setting up of little tracking stations on the islands?

Gallery: Yes, we had tracking stations all through the Caribbean.

Q: How much interest was manifested in this whole effort by the Navy brass, and by the Defense Department as a whole?

Gallery: It grew rather slowly at first. The interest was confined to a bunch of people who were regarded more or less as visionaries or dreamers, but as their dream began to take form a lot of people became convinced.

Eventually it resulted in such as the Polaris submarines.

Q: How did you happen to be assigned to that particular job? Were you considered a visionary and a dreamer?

Gallery: Maybe so. I was an ordnance P.G. for one thing. I think Radford had a lot to do with getting me assigned to that job because I knew him pretty well, and he was DCNO Air at that time, and I stood pretty well with him.

Q: Did you have a stable of scientists?

Gallery: No. I had a staff of eight or ten bright young officers. They were, all of them, very sharp characters. We didn't have any civilian scientists, no, but we had a lot of contacts on the outside.

Q: Was NOL in existance then? They had a stable of scientists.

Gallery: Yes, they had a lot.

Q: And they were doing something in the missile area or with atomic energy.

Gallery: They were just beginning to get into the missile field. At that time the Johns Hopkins outfit were our mainstay.

Gallery #4 - 141

Interview #4 with Rear Admiral Daniel V. Gallery, U.S. Navy
(Retired)

Place: U.S. Naval Institute, Annapolis, Maryland

Date: Wednesday morning, 26 July 1972

Subject: Biography

By: John T. Mason, Jr.

Q: Admiral, I'm very happy that you called and told me you were going to be in these parts today. It's always a pleasure to see you, Sir. Last time, you talked about the period from 1946 to 1949 when you were in the Navy Department and were concerned with guided missiles. Now, having reviewed the text, I think you have one or two items to add to that period.

Gallery: Yes. One thing I might mention is the so-called Gallery Memorandum, which I wrote while I was assistant CNO for guided missiles. It was addressed to the chief of naval operations and it was on the subject of the Navy's role in the future defense of the country. This was at the time of the big unification uproar when the Air Force was agitating to take over naval aviation, and of course this was a big item of interest to all naval aviators and all naval officers, for that matter.

So I wrote this memorandum to the chief of naval

operations. It was about a ten-page paper explaining what I thought was the Navy's role in the future, and it was quite different from the party line of the Defense Department at the time, which was Louis Johnson's party line, and it was quite controversial. Somehow or another - I don't know how - Drew Pearson got hold of this -

Q: One never knows how those people get hold of things!

Gallery: Right - and at that time the interservice bickering, so called, was a very hot subject. Drew Pearson ran this memo I think it was for three successive days. He printed the whole thing verbatim in his column, and it took him three days to get it all out. This, of course, started up quite a fuss around the Defense Department.

Q: Had this been a classified memo?

Gallery: Yes, it was "top secret," and it had been circulated by CNO among the deputies, and they had all commented on it, but that was all. Well, when this thing hit Drew Pearson's column there was a big flap about it. As I remember it, John L. Sullivan was Secretary of the Navy then and he took a very dim view of the matter and got very excited about it.

Q: He had seen it before its publication?

Gallery: I don't think he had, but all the Navy people did. John Dale Price, who was then deputy CNO - Sullivan had him in and raised hell with him about it, so John Dale sent me out of town on an inspection trip that would take about ten days.

Q: You were rather glad to -

Gallery: Yes, to get out of town until the heat came off. So, I left town and was gone for a week or ten days. That was the only thing to do, and the heat cooled off and by the time I got back Mr. Sullivan was worried about other things, but he had started the hell of an investigation to determine how this thing got out, but we never did find out.

Q: Did you have any suspicions?

Gallery: No, really, I don't know. I haven't any idea how it got out. An interesting sideline on it is - there were a number of copies of this memo made and I had to account for all the copies, and then, seven or eight years later, I wanted a copy of it. I had had to turn in my own copy at the time.

Gallery #4 - 144

Q: It was like a registered publication!

Gallery: Yes. Well, I wanted to get a copy of this thing, just for my own files, so I went to the CNO files and said I'd like to see a copy of the notorious Gallery Memorandum. They went all through their files and said there was no such thing in the files. Apparently, all copies of it were called in and destroyed, so there is no copy of the Gallery Memorandum in the CNO files now.

Q: The only place you can find it is in the newspaper files.

Gallery: In Drew Pearson's column. I have since gotten copies of his column, which I have gotten over here in the Library, in my files, which they have in the Library. Those are the only copies of the Gallery Memorandum. The ones that went to the CNO files have been destroyed.

Q: Did Senator Symington, who was then Secretary of Air, get involved in the thing?

Gallery: Oh, yes. Symington and I were, of course, at the opposite poles of this argument. I had one or two exchanges of correspondence with Symington, which were quite friendly and courteous, but on opposite sides of the question.

Q: You say that in this memo you took a different tack from the established line in the Department of Defense. Can you implement that?

Gallery: Yes. The main thing was this. At that time, the Air Force took the attitude that the future of warfare depended on strategic bombing, that a future war was going to be simply a strategic bombing war, blotting out cities, and that the atom bomb was the implement for doing that and the Air Force were the only ones who were entitled to deliver the atom bomb. Well, the theme of my memo was that the Navy was really better fitted to deliver the atom bomb than the Air Force was, on account of having carriers and submarines that could go anywhere in the world at sea and launch from them and we were better able to deliver the atom bomb than the Air Force which had to operate from land bases.

In view of later developments, the kind of carriers that we have now and particularly the Polaris submarines, what I said has turned out to be true. But at the time it was a very revolutionary doctrine because the general public were inclined to agree that the Air Force were the only ones who could deliver the atom bomb. So, as

I say, it was quite a controversial thing at that time.

Q: What was Pearson's objective in publishing that? Was it merely to keep the waters riled up?

Gallery: Yes, to stir up a fuss, and he did. He stirred up the hell of a fuss. This Gallery Memorandum and some of the articles I published, which also were controversial, got me tagged as a controversial character. A few years later I was eligible for three stars which I never made, and I'm sure that was the reason - I had been tagged controversial by that time, which was a very bad tag to get.

Q: It discourages one from expressing a point of view, doesn't it?

Gallery: Yes, in a way, but I think if I had to do it over again, I'd do the same thing.

Q: You said that the Secretary instituted an investigation to see how this thing got out. Were there any repercussions within the Defense Department? Was there any clamping down on security measures and that sort of thing, as a result of this episode? I'm thinking of the Pentagon Papers and the reaction to that.

Gallery: I don't know that anything actually happened. There was a lot of rumbling and bumbling in the front offices and Secretary of Defense Johnson issued some more directives about clearing things before they were published and about not making controversial public statements, and that sort of thing.

Q: But nothing comparable to the mess over the Pentagon Papers and their publication?

Gallery: No, it wasn't on that scale.

Q: That's an interesting thing to have included. Was there something else that pertained to that period, too?

Gallery: Let me see.

Q: Was there any idea germinating at that time, when you were in the Department, an idea which ultimately led to the Polaris project?

Gallery: Yes. We had a project to develop a missile which could be launched from a submarine.

Q: How did that idea originate?

Gallery: I don't know exactly how. It was just a natural development of the time. It just grew. We developed this drone - a guided drone which could be launched from a submarine and which had a range of about 400 miles. The sub had to surface to launch this thing. We developed that and actually fired it.

Q: Did it have a name?

Gallery: Yes, but it has escaped me right now. I may think of it later. This was the beginning, you might say, of the Polaris project because this was a guided missile that was launched by a submarine, and we developed it to a point where I think we had two or three submarines which were capable of launching this missile.

Q: Did you witness the launching yourself?

Gallery: Yes. We proved the thing. There was no doubt that it could be done because we'd done it. At that time there were experiments being conducted with launching a rocket from a submerged submarine. These were just at the very beginning at that time. That, you might say, was the beginning of the Polaris project - the surface-launch missile that we had plus the experiments with the submerged launch.

Q: Was the submerged launching considered much more feasible even in that embryonic state than the launching of the . . .

Gallery: It was considered much more desirable, of course, but it was not considered feasible at all at that time. Most of us thought that this underwater launch was impossible, but it turned out to be quite feasible.

Q: For what reasons did you think it was impossible?

Gallery: Well, it just had never been done and, looking at the thing off the top of your head, launching something underwater and having it pop out of the water and then go on its way just didn't seem feasible. But it turned out it was.

Q: Where did the Navy carry out these experiments? Was it at Canaveral - Cape Canaveral?

Gallery: Well, of course, that's where Polaris eventually wound up. I've forgotten where the experiments with the actual underwater launch were carried out.

Q: How much interest was demonstrated in the experiments

with missiles in the Navy itself? I mean, how much backing from the top brass did these experiments have?

Gallery: When I first took over as assistant CNO for guided missiles, I was the first one, and the fact that the Navy had established this job of assistant CNO for guided missiles indicates that there was an interest in the thing. The interest was, you might say, sort of academic. The Navy had enough interest in it to establish the office and to let us conduct some experiments. They didn't put much money in it. It was a distinct sideline at the time, but as we went on and actually developed some of these missiles and did things like launching a rocket from the Midway, which I told about in another interview, the interest developed. And later on - I guess six or seven years later - some of the things that we were doing eventually turned out to be the Polaris.

Q: Were the submarine boys interested particularly?

Gallery: Oh, yes. I had a submariner on my staff as the assistant CNO for guided missiles, Jack Ramage, who eventually got to be a vice admiral.

Q: You were in a unique position. You appreciate the

Gallery #4 - 151

value of public relations. Were you doing anything at that point to spread the gospel, so to speak?

Gallery: Yes, I was. That was one of my main jobs, public relations, and, as a matter of fact, the launching of the V-2 from the Midway, you might say, was mainly a public relations job because obviously we were never going to fire V-2 rockets from carriers like the Midway. But the Midway launch did generate a great deal of public attention and a great deal of interest.

Q: You told me last time about the Navy designating the Norton Sound as a very special converted ship. I guess she was a destroyer originally, wasn't she?

Gallery: A destroyer tender.

Q: I see. Anyway, she was converted and became a very special missile ship. Was she then put to good usage?

Gallery: Oh, yes, she was. She became our principal missile ship for quite a number of years, and that was a direct result of the Midway business, because after we'd launched the Midway with all the top brass out there, they went back to Washington and said, well, look, we can't afford to tie up something like the Midway for this sort of thing, but this is going to go

Gallery #4 - 152

on so we'll give you the Norton Sound.

Q: Did your job in those years take you away from Washington a great deal of the time?

Gallery: Yes, quite a lot. I had to go to White Sands, for instance, where the Army proving ground for missiles was. That's where I met Werner von Braun, for instance, in connection with the launching of a V-2. The V-2 was von Braun's baby, you know. He developed it in Germany and I had a talk with him about launching from the Midway. In fact, I believe he was out on the Midway to see the launch. And I had to go to Cape Canaveral, where we established what is now the principal launching ground for missiles. I was traveling a large part of the time, as a matter of fact.

Q: Admiral Raborn was not yet in the missile picture, was he?

Gallery: No.

Q: How did he come to get into that picture?

Gallery: I don't know actually how he got in. I think Admiral Arleigh Burke brought him in when the Polaris project was just starting and Burke gave him more or less dictatorial powers. He put him in charge of the project and told him that anything he wanted he could have. Raborn did a fabulous job, of course. He took over a project which many people regarded as visionary and which even the enthusiasts thought would take at least ten years to develop. Raborn actually put the whole thing together and had it working in half the scheduled time. It was just an absolutely fabulous job.

Raborn, incidentally, was my exec on the <u>Hancock</u> at the end of the war.

Q: He was?

Gallery: Yes.

Q: You must have worked very closely with the people in the Bureau of Ordnance, too, didn't you?

Gallery: Oh, yes.

Q: Who was that during your period in the Department?

Gallery: That was "Red" Schoeffel.

Q: And what about the AEC?

Gallery: I didn't have much real business to do with the AEC, but I knew Admiral Louis Strauss quite well. He's still a good friend of mine.

Q: Well, shall we go on to the next period then?

Gallery: All right.

Q: I think your next assignment was in charge of the operational development for the Atlantic Fleet. You served as deputy commander from November of 1949 to September of 1950. What did that entail?

Gallery: The operational development force was the outfit which took over new developments that had been worked up by the bureaus until they were satisfied with them, and then they would turn them over to the operational development force to take them to sea and test them to see whether they were as good as the bureaus who developed them claimed they were.

Q: That's the thing that Admiral Willis Lee set up?

Gallery: Lee? I don't remember that name.

Q: While World War II was still going on he was called

back from the Pacific to set up OpDevFor. Were there any new things that you tested in that development fleet?

Gallery: There's nothing in particular that sticks in my memory on that, no.

Q: You were stationed in Norfolk, weren't you?

Gallery: We were stationed in Norfolk, and we were testing new types of radar. None of these missiles had gotten to the stage where OpDevFor was concerned with them yet.

Q: You had the old battleship Mississippi down there, did you not?

Gallery: I think we did, yes.
   Then I went from there to Quonset Point and spent, I believe, five or six months as Commander, Fleet Air, Quonset, and then I went to sea again as Commander, Carrier Division Six, flying my flag in the Coral Sea, went to the Mediterranean and joined the Sixth Fleet under Admiral Gardner, who was then the commander of the Sixth Fleet. I spent a year in the Mediterranean as ComCarDiv Six.

Q: Can you recall any interesting experiences in that period?

Gallery: It was, for me, a very interesting time because I was the officer in technical command of the Sixth Fleet's aircraft carrier task force. Admiral Gardner let me run the show. He'd be along very often when we went to sea. His flagship was a cruiser but he'd turn over technical command to me and I'd run the exercises.

We went all through the Mediterranean from Gibraltar to Istanbul and Piraeus, Nice, Naples.

Q: We were virtually undisputed masters of the Mediterranean, weren't we?

Gallery: We certainly were. At that time, the Russians had nothing in the Mediterranean at all. We never saw a Russian ship. Never saw any Russian aircraft, either. We were absolutely undisputed masters of the Mediterranean.

Q: The Royal Navy was only there periodically, wasn't it?

Gallery: The Royal Navy was there and we saw quite a lot of them. We had exercises with them.

Q: What about the Italian Navy?

Gallery: There wasn't much of an Italian Navy then. Practically their whole fleet was in mothballs down in Taranto.

Q: A large part of duty in the Mediterranean was taken up with diplomatic functions and the like, wasn't it?

Gallery: Yes, it was a matter of going around and showing the flag in places like Istanbul and Piraeus, Naples.

Q: Keeping the Turks and the Greeks from each other!

Gallery: Yes. Well, the Sixth Fleet exercised quite an influence at that time in the Mediterranean.

Q: Did we use the facilities at Malta at all?

Gallery: Yes, we used it as a base for destroyers and sometimes our aircraft would land there. But we didn't use it too much because the Sixth Fleet at that time was developing the idea that they had no fixed base, that they operated entirely at sea, and refueled, re-provisioned, rearmed from ships at sea.

Q: What about repair problems?

Gallery: For repair, ships would come out to the Mediterranean, spend a year there, and then at the end of the year they'd go back to the States and be replaced by other ships. The idea was that the Sixth Fleet had no fixed base in the Mediterranean. They operated entirely at sea. They would go into port simply for diplomatic visits.

Q: Did we got into Spanish ports?

Gallery: Yes. We were quite friendly with the Spanish and, as a matter of fact, it was along about that time, I believe, that Admiral Forrest Sherman negotiated with Franco and we got Rota established.

Q: You wanted to describe a particular incident which had some effect.

Gallery: Yes. One day the <u>Coral Sea</u> was conducting air exercises and they sent a group of planes out in the morning to conduct exercises within 100 miles or so of the ship. It was a day when there was a low haze and clear and unlimited up high. Come noon, when all the planes were supposed to come back, there were two jets which didn't check in - didn't show up, and by the time they were fifteen minutes overdue we began to get worried about them. We finally got a call from one of the other planes circling over the ship saying that they had heard these two planes talking and they were lost and were going to have to land on the water pretty soon. And they said that these two planes thought they were about thirty or forty miles west of the ship, and they were going to go down on the water. We broke off a couple of destroyers, sent them out to the west, and sent other planes over there to look around for them. But we found nothing out there and we heard nothing more from these two planes that were lost. The only way we'd heard from them at all was indirectly through planes in the air hearing them talking and then relaying it back to the ship.

By about 12:30 we knew these planes were in the water, we couldn't find them thirty miles to the west of us, and so we were faced with a search problem and I decided to hit the panic button. We had just recently set up a large search and rescue business with all the NATO nations around the Mediterranean, where if you had a lost plane you could declare an emergency and everybody would join in the hunt for it, and I decided now is a good time to try out this new thing which we'd just set up. So, I hit the panic button and declared an emergency, and we got the Greeks, the French, the Italians, and the British. Their navies and air forces all joined in for the hunt. Of course, meantime I had launched our whole air group from the Coral Sea to search all around for these people and had also called in another carrier that we had out there and got them in it, and we spent the whole of the rest of this day looking for these lads but couldn't find them.

We began looking to the west because that's where they said they were going in, but eventually we worked our search to the east. We were, as I remember it, about four hundred miles west of Tel-Aviv. When nightfall came along, we had to recall our searching planes from the carriers and as soon as night set in then, the Gremlins got busy. By that time all the merchant ships in the Mediterranean had been cut in on the thing and they began sighting strange lights all over the Mediterranean blinking SOS. Some of them reported sighting life rafts with people in them. Some of the air force planes reported lights. In fact, all during the night we had a continual stream of reports, each one of which taken by itself, indicated that they'd found these guys and we can follow up now. But each one of them turned out to be a false alarm.

When it came dawn the next day, the sun came up, and all the Gremlins disappeared - nothing.

Then, later that afternoon, we finally found these two guys. They had gone in the water about three hundred miles to the east of us. They claimed they were going in thirty miles to the west. Actually, they went in three hundred miles to the east. We found out that what had happened was that they had gone out on a gunnery mission, which would take a couple of hours, to the west of the ship a hundred miles or so, and they hadn't kept very close track of where they were and when they started home they were flying over this haze and they couldn't see the water, but it was perfectly clear up where they were. So, to get back to the ship, they turned on their homers and they were going to home on a beacon that we had on the Coral Sea. Well, as it turned out, we found out later, they had a homing beacon at Tel-Aviv which was on almost exactly the same frequency as the one that we had on the Coral Sea. And, it so happened that the call letters of the Coral Sea and the call letters of the homing beacon at Tel-Aviv were almost identical. In the Morse code there were series of about a dozen dots and dashes and they were identical, except for one dot which was easy enough to confuse. So, these lads had tuned in the Tel-Aviv station which was almost the same frequency. They listened and got what they jumped to the conclusion was our call. There was just one dot difference. And so they went to work and homed on Tel-Aviv. They went right over the ship but didn't see us, and then just kept going, kept going, kept going till they ran out of gas and landed in the water, got out their rafts, the planes sank and they spent twenty-four hours paddling around the water till we found them.

Q: Did our forces find them or did the NATO forces?

Gallery: Our forces from the <u>Coral Sea</u> finally found them three hundred miles to the east.

Q: How do you account for all those false reports that occurred during the night?

Gallery: Just imagination! That was quite an interesting and exciting time. We got the boys back.

Q: After your period of duty in the Mediterranean, you transferred to the Atlantic itself, didn't you?

Gallery: Yes. I came back from the Mediterranean and I was given command of the Hunter-Killer Force, Atlantic, which had just been organized and, at the time, we had a couple of jeep carriers in it. I had that for, I believe, six or seven months.

Q: This was under the commander-in-chief of the Atlantic?

Gallery: Yes.

Q: Did it involve NATO forces as well?

Gallery: No, it was purely an American force.

Q: Tell me about that. I mean, what were your objectives and what exercises did you engage in?

Gallery: The Hunter-Killer Force had just been organized and it was, you might say, a development of the Hunter-Killer Groups which we had in the Atlantic during the war which were based on jeep carriers, and these were jeep carriers that we had in the Hunter-Killer Force.

Q: A concept you understood very well because you helped develop it!

Gallery: Yes. That later developed into <u>Essex</u>-class carriers instead of jeeps, because after all the jeeps were marginal. They were very small and they had no speed and they bounced around a lot in a seaway, so taking off and landing from them was very difficult, and eventually the jeeps were replaced by <u>Essex</u>-class carriers, and that's what we have now - we're using big carriers for hunter-killer work.

Q: There's no question now, as there was no question in the early fifties, about night operations?

Gallery: There's no question, now, it's routine now, but in the early fifties it still was pretty much of an adventure. We started it during the war. In fact, I think I told about starting it in the Atlantic.

Q: This was what prompted my remark. You told about it very graphically, about the development of this.

Gallery: Yes, well, I would say that at this time everyone realized that it was possible, but it was still an adventure. It isn't any more. It's routine now.

Q: It was still an adventure in the early fifties because the equipment wasn't what it is now?

Gallery: ~~Yes. Well,~~ they were still operating from jeeps, and now they're operating from a 50,000-ton ship with a canted deck, which is just the difference between night and day.

After four or five months in the Hunter-Killer Force,

I went to Glenview, Illinois, as commander of naval air reserve training.

Q: Was this something you had sought?

Gallery: No, I didn't ask for it but I was glad to get it, and I put in four and a half very fine years there.

Q: Tell me about that training command.

Gallery: Naval air training?

Q: Yes, the scope of the program.

Gallery: At that time we had twenty-eight naval air reserve stations scattered all over the whole country. This was the so-called weekend warriors' outfit, where reserve people would come in every weekend and fly training missions in the airplanes. And they proved themselves, incidentally. In the Korean War we recalled a large number of them and they performed very finely in the Korean War.

Q: By and large, what was the background of these reserves?

Gallery: They had been regular Navy pilots in World War II and after the war they joined the Naval Reserve and they would come in every weekend - one weekend a month, rather - and fly our planes. In that way, they were able to keep themselves ready for deployment in case of emergency.

Q: How did you handle new recruits?

Gallery: Well, new recruits came in from the fleet. As people finished their tour of duty in the regular Navy and were discharged, they would then join the Naval Reserve, and we were getting quite a large number of people to join the reserve and keep up their flying.

Q: What inducements did you offer? What kind of a program of publicity?

Gallery: I've always thought that there were several things that induced them to come. One, they got paid for it a little bit, but the pay was entirely incidental because there were many of those lads who spent more money coming to weekend drill and getting home again than they got for going to the drill. So that was entirely incidental. Another thing was that they had bird blood in their veins and they liked to fly. And then another thing was that they liked to associate with others who spoke the language and to get back in the Navy for a while and rub elbows with people who spoke the Navy language. This was another thing that attracted them. The final thing, and I'm sure this was one of the main things, was simply patriotism. We had a large and growing outfit at that time.

One of the main parts of my job was to circulate around this command, which covered the whole country, and inspect the groups. Once a year I would get round to each one of the twenty-eight stations and conduct a formal review and inspection.

Q: Approximately how many men would you have at a given time involved in this reserve program?

Gallery: Oh, let me see. The biggest station was out at Los Angeles where we had about 5,000. I might be way off on this, but I would estimate we had on the order of 60,000 people in the program altogether. The main stations were New York, Philadelphia, Chicago, Los Angeles. Those were the four big ones, but we had them scattered all over.

Q: Was it possible for a man to come in to the Naval Reserve training program from civilian life without prior naval service as a background?

Gallery: For the enlisted men it was. Of course, to be a pilot you had to go to Pensacola and get your wings. So they had to have prior naval service, but we could take enlisted men in direct from civilian life.

Q: And how large a segment of the total number were enlisted men?

Gallery: I would say twenty enlisted men to one officer.

Q: And they were the mechanics and the maintenance people?

Gallery: Yes.

Q: Did you use the newest Navy planes for training purposes?

Gallery: We didn't have the latest, no, but we had modern airplanes. We had quite a number of jets, and we had all types of planes, transports, bombers, jet fighters, antisub planes.

Gallery #4 - 169

Q: Did you have formal classes for instruction at these various unit bases?

Gallery: Yes.

Q: What sort of courses did you offer there?

Gallery: It would depend on what the mission of the squadron was. Each squadron would have its own classes dealing with their particular type of plane and their particular mission.

Q: I meant would it involve instruction in weather and that sort of thing, as well as supplementary subjects to the flying?

Gallery: Yes.

Q: Communications and what have you?

Gallery: Yes. I remember, incidentally, one inspection I made out at Santa Ana in California. This was, as I say, our biggest station. I think we had 5,000 people in ranks that day, and Vice President Nixon came to the inspection. There had just recently been an article in the newspaper saying that Nixon, who was a naval reserve, had just been notified by the Bureau of Personnel that he was eligible for promotion, I think to the rank of commander, except that he had not attended enough drills in the past year and therefore he couldn't make it. So Nixon came to our inspection at Santa Ana and was going to talk to the troops afterwards. At these inspections they always brought their families and made a big show of the thing, and then they'd have a speech afterwards by somebody, and Nixon was going to speak to the boys. We had Nixon go round with us on the inspection. He accompanied me as I went up and down the ranks, you know.

So, when I introduced him, I said that we had Vice President Nixon here today and, as many of them knew from the newspapers, he had just been notified by the Bureau of Personnel that he was not eligible for promotion because he had not attended enough drills. I said, now, all of you have seen that he has attended drill today and that we put him to work, he has helped me inspect here, so I am going to notify the Bureau of Personnel about this and make sure that he gets credit for attending this inspection. Well, Nixon got quite a kick out of this.

A week or so later, I got a very stuffy letter from the Bureau of Personnel saying that they considered it was improper for me to do this!

Q: It wasn't in the Regs?

Gallery: Yes.

Q: Your headquarters was at Glenview, Illinois. Is that on Lake Michigan?

Gallery: It's right on the lake. It's about ten miles north of The Loop, just north of Evanston.

Q: You also wore another hat at that time. You were commander of the Ninth Naval District. What did that entail?

Gallery: Yes. I was - let's see, it was Admiral "Pop" Olds who was commander of the Naval District. He retired and they didn't have anybody at the time available to replace him, so they gave me the extra job of filling in for about six months. So, for six months, I had to shuttle back and forth between Glenview and Great Lakes.

Q: What are the principal duties in the Ninth Naval District? Do they involve the Great Lakes Training Center itself?

Gallery: Great Lakes Training Center is more or less

the headquarters. The Naval District, of course, covers all the central part of the country. They were just the regular duties of a naval district commander, a large part of which was public relations.

After about six months Admiral Savvy Forrestal came in and relieved me of that job.

Incidentally, it was during my tour at Glenview that we brought the U-505 to Chicago, but I think I've already covered that.

Q: You've already told me about that, yes, about all the vicissitudes of getting it there.

This training program was a vitally important part of the total Navy program.

Gallery: Yes, it is and, as I say, it proved itself in the Korean War when we had to re-call quite a number of naval reserves back and they performed very creditably indeed.

Q: Were there any innovations during your period there? I mean any things that you initiated? New techniques?

Gallery: No, I don't think so.

Q: I can't conceive of this not happening!

Gallery: Well, there were a few changes in some of our programs for attracting new recruits and that sort of thing.

Q: For instance?

Gallery: That's going back a long way and my recollection of that sort of thing is getting a little sketchy.

Q: Did you have a virtually free hand in the development of this training program? Or did Washington keep an eagle eye on the whole thing?

Gallery: My boss was the commander of naval air training.

Q: That was Fitz Lee?

Gallery: That was originally John Dale Price, and then later Admiral Artie Doyle. Their headquarters was down at Pensacola. They were the only ones who really checked up on me and they didn't check up much. It was practically an independent command, I'd say.

Q: Tell me about Artie Doyle. Did you have close contact with him?

Gallery: Oh, yes. I'd known Artie a long, long time. I couldn't tell you about Artie Doyle in five minutes, or in five hours, for that matter. Artie was quite a guy.

Q: I know that, and that's why I asked about him.

Gallery: As I say, I've known Artie ever since the Naval Academy. I remember when he was at sea he had a habit of deflating some skipper who thought very well of himself by sending him a message and instead of saying, well done, he would say fairly well done!

Gallery #5 - 175

Interview #5 with Rear Admiral Daniel V. Gallery, U.S. Navy
(Retired)

Place: His home in Oakton, Virginia

Date: Monday afternoon, 16 September 1974

Subject: Biography

By: John T. Mason, Jr.

Q: Well, Sir, it's great to see you again after our grievous error in ruining that previous tape when you talked very well about your period -

Gallery: Very suspicious to have tapes ruined these days, you know!

Q: It certainly is. This was not only an 18-minute erasure but a total one!

Well, Sir, last time, you ended your remarks by talking about the period when you were commander of the Ninth Naval District in Chicago. I believe it was on December 6, 1956, that you left there, left that command, to take command of the Caribbean Sea Frontier?

Gallery: Yes.

Q: Tell me about the Caribbean Sea Frontier. What was the scope of that?

Gallery: The geographical limits are the Gulf of Mexico down to Panama and the Caribbean. It's a joint command. In other words, it involves Army, Navy, and Air Force, and I was the senior commander of the whole bunch. In addition to the Caribbean Sea Frontier, I was also the commandant of the Tenth Naval District, which is part of the shore establishment of the Navy.

Q: And your base was in San Juan?

Gallery: My base was in San Juan. The Caribbean Sea Frontier is a naval command. I think I said it was a joint command. It's not, it's a naval command, and that takes in the Caribbean and the Gulf, but I was also the Antilles Defense Commander and that is a joint command.

Q: That's all three services?

Gallery: That's all three services, so I had three hats.

Q: That's a joint command similar to CinCLant, is it?

Gallery: CinCLant wouldn't be a joint command.

Q: No. Similar to CinCPac.

Gallery: Yes.

Q: So you wore three hats?

Gallery: Yes, I had three hats, Antilles Defense Command, Caribbean Sea Frontier, and Tenth Naval District.

Q: Does that mean you had three staffs?

Gallery: No, just one staff.

Now, theoretically, it was up to me to look out for American interests throughout the Caribbean and Central America, but actually I could do very little on my own hook. The State Department was looking over my shoulder all the time and I couldn't make a move without an okay from the State Department. It was very seldom that I saw eye to eye with the State Department.

Q: I might ask what were, in general, American interests in the area for which you had a concern?

Gallery: Well, such things as when Vice President Nixon visited South America, and he almost got lynched, you know, in Venezuela. I was interested in protecting him and getting him out. At that time we set up a rescue operation - this hasn't been publicized - consisting of a good-sized airlift of military personnel and tanks and vehicles to fly down and land in Venezuela, go in from the airport to the American consulate, where Nixon was being held safely, and pick him up and take him from the consulate to the airport, put him on a plane and get him out. We were all set to do that. We came within an ace of doing it.

Q: The forces would have gone from Puerto Rico, would they?

Gallery: Some of them were at Ramey, which is in Puerto Rico. Others were in the United States. But this whole task force was mobilized and ready to go on an instant's notice. Eventually they got Nixon out without using it. I was there to meet him when he landed in Puerto Rico from Venezuela. When he got out of the plane that night his eyes were as big as golf balls. I was rather proud of him and the way he had conducted himself because it was a close thing. He could have been physically harmed and maybe even killed.

Well, that was one thing. I don't think we cut the State Department in on that rescue operation at all because that was the sort of thing that they threw up their hands in holy horror about. Anyway, we set it up but we didn't use it.

Another thing came up while I was there involving the State Department, and that was Castro. Castro at that time was a rebel in the hills of Oriente and the State Department was backing him - Castro is our man, we put him in, with the State Department's blessing.

Q: He was a agrarian reformer!

Gallery: Yes. You may remember his people kidnapped thirty of my sailors from Guantanamo who had gone on liberty up to Guantanamo City on a Saturday night. They were coming back on a bus and four of his guerrillas from the hills stopped the bus, boarded it with rifles, and simply kidnapped these thirty sailors and took them up into the hills and held them for two or three weeks.

Q: This wasn't an accident?

Gallery: Accident? Hell, no. This was deliberate. They kidnapped the sailors on the bus.

When this happened I wanted to send the Marines up into the hills to release these boys. Arleigh Burke went along with me, but the State Department would have none of it. They said, "you'd bring out nothing but dead men." I didn't believe that because if Castro had killed our sailors, the Marines would have wiped out Castro and his whole damned band. It would be a lot different world, too, if we had. Anyway, the State Department said, "No, no, you let us negotiate." So I let them negotiate and after about two weeks of negotiation they sent our boys back.

I was at Guantanamo when they got back. There were thirty of them, mind you, and it was only four of Castro's mob that kidnapped them, and among the thirty there wasn't a single broken bone, there wasn't a black eye, there wasn't a mark on a damned one of them. They didn't put up any sort of resistance whatever.

Q: Had they been well taken care of while they were in captivity?

Gallery: Oh, yes, they were treated all right, but I took a dim view of their putting up no resistance whatever, which they didn't. They just went right along with them.

Q: Of course, they were not armed at that point, were they?

Gallery: No, they were not armed, but, hell, there were thirty to four. One trouble was, of course, that they were coming back from Guantanamo City on a Saturday night and most of them were half-drunk.

Anyway, that's another case where I didn't see eye to eye with the State Department.

Q: But where the State Department stepped in and said, "we want to do so and so" this took precedence over the military?

Gallery: Yes. Of course, I was taking my orders from Arleigh Burke and Arleigh was in favor of it but he said, "I'll have to get this okayed by the State Department," and the State Department told Arleigh to lay off, so he told me to lay off and that was that. Now, had we gone ahead and gone up and gotten those boys, I think the history of the Caribbean would be quite different, because as things turned out you can't blame Castro for being contemptuous of the United States. Hell, here he comes along and kidnaps thirty of our sailors and all we do is say tut, tut, and they returned them to us in two weeks. So why should he have any respect for us when we put up with that sort of thing? If we'd gone ahead and got them, it would have been a different story.

I had a constant stream of VIP visitors that I had to entertain down there, the Secretary of the Navy, the

Deputy Chief of Naval Operations, Jim Hagerty, the President's press secretary, and several other White House functionaries came down.

Q: And I suppose congressional junkets, too?

Gallery: Some congressmen, yes. You see, I had a guest house there where I could put them up for as long as they wanted to stay. Among other visitors, I had a lot of distinguished visitors, there was the heir-apparent to the throne of Spain and then his son, who is actually going to be the next king of Spain probably. They came down and visited a while. Winston Churchill came in on the Onassis yacht. I was invited out to lunch on board. When I went aboard I took one of my books along and autographed it to Winston.

Q: What book did you take? *Eight Bells*?

Gallery: I think it was *Eight Bells*, but I'm not sure. I presented it to him which, of course, sort of put him on the spot and he had to give me one of his books, which he signed for me.

Q: What did he give you?

Gallery: One of his early books. When I told many of my friends around San Juan about this swap of books, many of them claimed that this was the greatest swindle ever perpetrated in the history of English literature.

Q: Why?

Gallery: Well, as long as they didn't specify who swindled whom, I let it go at that.

Mrs. Churchill was there and I asked her if she would like to see an American baseball game because it was during spring training when some of the big league ball clubs were down in Puerto Rico training. She said she would, so I took her over to the ball park. I had the key to the governor's box, I used to go to a lot of the ball games and watch them from the governor's box.

Q: Was that Munoz Marin?

Gallery: Yes. I took Mrs. Churchill there and two big league teams were playing. There was quite a big crowd and about the third inning - I was in my white uniform and Mrs. Churchill is a very distinguished-looking old gal - everyone in the grandstand knew me and they put two and two together and soon realized that this was Mrs. Churchill and the word got around. We watched the game till about the seventh inning and Mrs. Churchill got quite a kick out of it -

Q: Did she understand it?

Gallery: Yes, apparently. We got up to go in the seventh inning, the game was in progress, and, as we were leaving the park, the umpire stopped the game and all hands in the ball park gave Mrs. Churchill a standing ovation. She got a big bang out of that.

Q: When VIPs came to visit your command, did you have a routine, did you have special things that you demonstrated, or what?

Gallery: No, I wouldn't say I had any special routine because their interests were quite different. I would, for instance, offer to take them fishing for tarpon and most of them would take me up on that. If we had a nuclear submarine in I'd offer to give them a ride in that, but I let them tell me what they wanted rather than try to anticipate their needs.

Q: What kind of ships did you have under your command?

Gallery: Actually, I had nothing under my command as

Commander, Caribbean Sea Frontier, except a few tugboats and minesweepers, but there would always be a large number of Atlantic Fleet ships down there training at Roosevelt Roads. Especially during the winter months, we'd have a large part of the Atlantic Fleet right down there. They didn't actually come under my command, except when the boys were ashore.

Q: Then they were under your command?

Gallery: Yes.

Q: Did that entail problems in discipline when you had them ashore?

Gallery: It could very well have because at times, especially during the winter when there was a big fleet delegation in, we'd have maybe 5,000 or 10,000 sailors dumped ashore in San Juan, which is a place where there are plenty of opportunities to get in trouble. But I was on very good terms with Dona Felicia, who was the mayoress of San Juan. She was a fabulous character and whenever the fleet came in she would throw a big party at the City Hall, get all the good-looking girls in town to the party, and the sailors would come and get acquainted. When sailors were detailed to go to this party most of them took a dim view of it, you know, "what the hell, this is just a party, but we've got to go and that's that." But when they got there and had a look at these girls it was different.

That was one thing. Then Dona Felicia issued instructions to her police force that their job was to keep sailors out of trouble rather than to get them in trouble. We didn't have a single serious incident all the time I was there, thanks largely to Dona Felicia's cooperation.

Q: What was your relationship with Governor Marin?

Gallery: Very good.

Q: Tell me about him.

Gallery: Actually, I didn't have a great deal to do with him, except socially. He'd have me out to dinner now and then and I'd have him, but we had very little official business. Most of the official business I had was with Dona Felicia, but Marin was a very fine man. He was one of the great statesmen of Latin America, and under his regime Puerto Rico made very great strides. It came up from being the poorhouse of North America to a show place. The State Department was sending people down to show them what the United States was doing.

Gallery #5 - 187

Q: Was this in the time of Bootstrap?

Gallery: Yes, Operation Bootstrap was in full swing then and was accomplishing great things.

Q: Also, we did things in an agricultural sense, didn't we? We taught them how to take care of their land?

Gallery: Yes, but the main thing was that we sort of weaned them from a sugar economy, that's what they were, we weaned them away from that to an industrial economy.

Q: From a one-crop economy to industry?

Gallery: Yes.

Q: Talk about Vieques and Roosevelt Roads and the use of Puerto Rican facilities by the U.S. Navy.

Gallery: I would say at least half of the island of Vieques was in use constantly by the Marines. They used it for firing live ammunition. It was in constant use. The Marines had many landing exercises there.
    Culebra was just starting up when I was there but it's gotten a lot of publicity since then. We had a firing range on Culebra, too, which the ships would

shoot at. Very few people lived on Culebra but those who did objected to the use of the island, and I think we have now abandoned it although I'm not sure. That would have occurred after my time.

Q: There wasn't much agitation when you were there?

Gallery: No, there wasn't.

Q: There wasn't a nationalistic movement in Puerto Rico when you were there, either, was there?

Gallery: Well, there were the Independistas, who were wild-eyes radicals, and they were in favor of independence for Puerto Rico, but they were very, very small minority, less than one percent. Then there was one party that favored statehood and the other favored Munoz Marin and his people favored the commonwealth. Ferre was head of the statehood party. If I had been a Puerto Rican I think I would have favored Munoz Marin and his commonwealth deal because, well, they got all the best of that because they have American citizenship and they don't pay any American taxes. They've got all the privileges of citizenship and very few of the responsibilities. So I think I'd be in favor of that!

Q: Except that with statehood they'd have a freer flow

of goods, wouldn't they, back and forth?

Gallery: I'm not sure what all the arguments for statehood are, but Luis Ferre, who defeated Munoz Marin for governor, was in favor of statehood and could address lots of strong arguments for it. But I don't know what they were.

Q: Did your command have anything to do with the OAS?

Gallery: No. Well, we had relations with all the countries involved in it, but not with the OAS as such.

Q: No Navy setup with them at all?

Gallery: No.

Q: What about Central America when you were there?

Gallery: I don't remember that we had any incidents in Central America.

Q: This was before the exodus of Cubans to Florida and Central America because of Castro, wasn't it?

Gallery: Yes.

Q: He had yet to gain control?

Gallery: Yes.

Q: What precisely, as Commander of the Antilles Defense Command, did this entail? The British islands in the Caribbean? Were you involved there?

Gallery: The Antilles Defense Command was a purely American setup involving the Army, Navy, and Air Force of the United States.

Q: But since we had bases in various of those islands in the Caribbean, did this entail involvement with those islands, like Antigua, for instance?

Gallery: I don't recall we had one in Antigua. We had a base in Trinidad and so I had relations with the government of Trinidad for that reason. Trinidad's about the only one, except that we did have some small communications set up on various islands, but those were fairly small things.

I had various interests while I was down there. One was the Navy League and while I was down there I helped the Navy League all I could and they grew to be the strongest chapter in the whole United States. By the time I left there it was bigger than the one in New

York.

Q: It was in the island of Puerto Rico?

Gallery: Yes.

Q: Was there a chapter in Panama, too?

Gallery: I think so, but I don't know. Puerto Rico was my main interest, and that was very strong.

Q: What did you do to increase the membership? How did you promote this?

Gallery: I made each member of the Navy League an honorary member of the Officers' Club in San Juan, which had a hell of a big influence, because the Officers' Club is a very nice place and they got drinks there a lot cheaper than they could get them elsewhere. It was a very popular place and that was quite an attraction. I have since been informed that this thing was strictly illegal.

Q: Why?

Gallery: Well, the Navy Department viewed it with alarm and I hadn't asked the Navy Department whether I could do it or not. I just figured I could. Eventually, it turned out I couldn't, but by that time we had the biggest Navy League in the country.

Q: But what harm would there be in organizing one and promoting one?

Gallery: I don't know, but there are always people sniping at various privileges you have like the Officers' Club, the commissary, and various other things.

Q: Oh, I see. That was the angle that they objected to. But you didn't get reprimanded for it?

Gallery: No, I got out before they found out about it!

Q: What happened after you left?

Gallery: They made them knock it off.

Q: Did this mean that the Navy League chapter diminished?

Gallery: It did, yes. It diminished some, but it's still quite strong.

Another interest while I was down there was my steel band. I knew nothing about steel bands until shortly after I got there. I went down to Trinidad for an inspection and I was there at carnival time.

Q: Mardi Gras.

Gallery: Trinidad is where steel drums originated. In case you don't know, a steel band consists of instruments that are all empty 50-gallon oil drums.

Q: I like the music of steel bands.

Gallery: You've heard them?

Q: Oh, yes.

Gallery: The first time I heard a steel drum was at carnival time in Trinidad, and the music just got inside me and shook me up. So I ordered a set of drums from the best drum-maker in Trinidad and then I came back to San Juan and got hold of my bandmaster and told him that I had ordered a set of drums and I wanted him to teach his boys to play them. Well, the bandmaster had never heard of steel drums either, so I told him what they were, and he looked at me as if I were a nut. But, being a good Navy chief, he said, aye, aye, Sir.

He told me later that he had just finished twenty

years and he figured, what the hell, I can retire any time I want to and if this thing doesn't turn out I'll just retire.

About two weeks later word came up from Trinidad that the drums were ready, so I sent the chief and band down to Trinidad to pick them up, and to spend about a week there rubbing elbows with the local musicians to learn how to play them.

When the word got around the waterfront in Trinidad that a bunch of Navy sailors were down there learning to play steel drums in a week, all the local musicians laughed like hell and said it can't be done. Only a native can play a steel drum.

Q: Only a native had that sense of rhythm.

Gallery: Yes. Well, at the end of a week my boys had a pretty good beat going. And so just before coming back to San Juan, the Chief sent for some of the local musicians to come out to the Naval Station and listen to the boys play. They were playing in a hangar, and they blasted off with "Carnival Road March" and "Happy Wanderer" and such things. They were real good and the jaws of all the local musicians popped right open. Roper, my Chief, had a blackboard in the hangar on which he had written the parts for the six different drums - different kinds of drums. One of the local musicians finally looked up at the blackboard and saw the parts up there and he said, "Oh, hell, you guys can read music. Unfair competition."

Q: Most of them don't read music.

Gallery: No, they can't read music at all.
   Anyway, those boys came back to San Juan and eventually they got to be the best steel band in the Caribbean. The natives are very good and they've got a real sense of rhythm but my boys had that too and, in addition, my boys were musicians - and they could read music.

Q: They were disciplined, too.

Gallery: Yes, and besides that - this was a big thing - Roper, my Chief, could arrange the parts. The natives have to find it out by experiment.

Q: Harmonizing?

Gallery: Yes, but Roper would sit down and visualize all this stuff and write it out for them. They got to be real good and eventually they went to the World's Fair in Brussels. I have a picture of them there.

Q: They stole the show in Brussels!

Gallery: Yes.

Q: They were in the American Pavilion?

Gallery: In the American Pavilion, which was right next to the Russian Pavilion. They played four concerts a day and whenever they did they would empty the Russian Pavilion. Eventually, the Russians sent over a camera crew with tape recorders and they canned the whole business. I've been expecting ever since to have the Russians claim that they originated the steel band, but I haven't heard it yet.

Q: That's where Catherine Howard came into the picture, I guess. She was in charge of the American Pavilion. Remember her?

Gallery: No. I don't remember her.

Q: She was the President's special representative.

Gallery: We played there a week and at the end of the week the man in charge of the American show there talked to the White House on the telephone and demanded that we stay another week and we did. We were the only show the whole summer that was held over.

Q: Were you in uniform?

Gallery: Yes. When they first told me that I could send the band to Brussels, I told them, "They should be accompanied by a flag officer who knows all about steel drums. I don't give a damn who you send, but he must know something about steel drums." So they said, okay, you can go.

Q: Tell me about the name that they used, this steel band of yours?

Gallery: The boys made it up themselves. Admiral Dan's Pandemoniacs, they called themselves. They got to be quite famous and very much in demand. They were wanted at numerous state fairs, lots of Navy parties all around the States, and eventually they got traveling so much keeping these engagements that the wives of the boys began complaining to me and said, "Now, look, these boys are supposed to be on shore duty but they're away more than if they were on a ship," which was true. Anyway, they were very much in demand.

Q: Also, you lost the services of your band for the most part, didn't you?

Gallery: Yes, but we could stand that. They were doing a lot of good. They made a good will tour of South America, for instance, and this was after the Nixon lynching business and the State Department was very leery of it when they heard of it. At first they took a dim view of it and said no, don't send them. Then they said, well, all right, you can go, but play only in opera houses or in the main public square of the town. Keep the boys out of the slum areas because they'll get mobbed.

So we sent them on the tour and they played everywhere, including the slum areas, and just like the State Department said, they got mobbed in the slum areas for autographs. They did more good on that trip than years and years of State Department parties could ever do.

Q: They reached the people.

Gallery: Yes, they got to the people. We had one boy who could speak good Spanish and explain the whole thing.

Q: Incidentally, how's your Spanish?

Gallery: I neglected it, I'm sorry to say.

I had another interest while I was down there, a little league. Of course, you had all sorts of - there were plenty of youngsters in San Juan and you have good weather all year round for baseball, and baseball is a very popular sport. So I introduced a little league while I was there. I organized a total of twenty leagues, each league consisting of four teams, so that was eighty teams we had.

Q: In the island?

Gallery: Yes. It's now up to one hundred and some. It's still going on. They didn't have any such thing at all when I first got there. I got it going and I would go around to various businessmen in town and put the bite on them for $1,500 to start a league. That's what it cost to buy uniforms, bats, balls, and so on. And I got twenty leagues started. It was very successful.

Q: Did Navy personnel assist in these leagues?

Gallery: No, but the Navy came into it to this extent. We'd have - we had four Little League fields on the Naval Station, where the teams could come in and play. We also had fields around town here, there, and everywhere but we didn't have enough to go round so we made up four fields on the Naval Station and they'd come in there and play. I used to get around each weekend and see most of them playing. The Puerto Ricans take their baseball very, very seriously indeed and I had to arbitrate numerous arguments which sometimes got pretty violent, and at times I would have to confiscate the game, as they say.

Q: Confiscate it?

Gallery: That's forfeit the game. Whenever I did I needed a squad of Marines to escort me off the field when it was over. They would get very violent at the time but after they'd had time to cool off and think it over, it would be all right. They realized I was the same kind of SOB to everybody and so long as I was they could take it.

I was the commissioner for Little League baseball for Latin America, which took in Venezuela, Panama, and Mexico, as well as Puerto Rico. The first year that I was there Puerto Rico won the Latin American championship and went up to Williamsport and played in the World Series.

Q: This took you to these other countries, to Mexico and Venezuela?

Gallery: Yes.

Q: How did you tie that in with your Navy duties?

Gallery: I don't remember now but I could find reasons for it.

Q: Did the State Department approve of this operation?

Gallery: I didn't cut them in on it!

I think that just about covers what I have to say. No, wait a minute, I'm not through yet.

Q: I've got another question to ask you. In Puerto Rico also there's something else of great note and that's the annual Casals Music Festival. You had something to do with that, too, did you not?

Gallery: Well, no, nothing except be a listener.

Q: Did you get to know Pablo Casals?

Gallery: Yes, I did get to know him. As a matter of fact, I invited him over to hear a rehearsal by my steel band. I had my fingers crossed, of course, when I invited him over, for a famous musician like Pablo Casals to listen to a bunch of sailors hammering on empty oil drums! But Pablo came and he went into orbit over the band. He thought it was wonderful and at the end of it he went around tapping on the drums, put his ear down and listened to them, and he said, "Now, these drums have a pure musical note which is not matched by anything in the symphony." He asked me if he could borrow a set of my bass drums, which were down in the same range as the cello is, you know, to try out in his symphony. I told him he was welcome to, but I left before we got around to doing that.

Anyway, when he came to listen to our rehearsal one of the pieces that we played for him, just to show off as a matter of fact, was the Poet and Peasant Overture. Now, that's a very ambitious piece of music, and the boys played it absolutely perfectly for Casals. They'd been rehearsing it for about three months and I used to go down and listen to them once a week at least. They never were able to get through it perfectly. There was always some foul-up here, there, or everywhere. But, for Casals, it was absolutely perfect, and at the end of it the boys just stopped. Casals jumped up to his feet and started clapping. He thought it was fine.

Q: Did the steel band continue after you left?

Gallery: It's still going on, yes. I heard them just a couple of months ago. They have a constant turnover of personnel, of course, but they keep training new men, and they're still very good.

In 1960 I was scheduled to be transferred from Puerto Rico and I still had two years to go before I would retire for age and grade. So I was slated for a job in Germany as a military advisor, which I looked forward to very much. But at the last minute the Army indulged in some sort of skullduggery in which they managed to get the job made an Army job instead of a Navy job, so that went up the spout. There was no other job I wanted for which I was eligible at the time and while they were trying to make up their minds where they would send me the doctors found me physically disabled with emphysema. So I retired in November of 1960, after over forty years of active naval service.

This retirement came up rather suddenly and they asked me if I wanted to have a retirement ceremony at the Navy Yard with some guards and bands and guns firing a salute. The time was so short that I really wouldn't have had time to invite any of my friends to it, so I told them no. I'm sorry now that I didn't let them blow the bugles and shoot the guns, but anyway I just retired.

You might think that after forty-some years of active service, most of it pretty active, you might think when you retire, well, maybe somewhere along the line I did something I'll be remembered for. And I did a thing or two, such as being on the 1920 Olympic team, flying Navy airplanes of all kinds for over thirty years, boarding and capturing a German submarine, and writing numerous books and articles. But if you asked almost anybody on active duty around Washington today, Do you know Dan Gallery? Do you know what they'll say, "Yes, he's the guy who started that steel band down in San Juan."

There's a moral to that story somewhere, but I don't know what!

Q: Would you pause for a moment and talk a little about your experience as a flyer? You have over 6,000 hours to your credit and you've flown all sorts of planes from the very primitive types to the jets.

Gallery: That's right.

Q: Talk a little about that, will you?

Gallery: Well, when I started flying, the planes that we flew were primitive compared to what they have now. We had fixed landing gear instead of retractable. They were mostly biplanes with wire between the wings which gave you a built-in head wind, no flaps, no brakes, a tail skag instead of a tail wheel.

Gallery #5 - 205

Q: No parachutes?

Gallery: No, no, we had parachutes. Fixed propeller instead of adjustable flaps. When I started, the normal cruising speed of the planes that we flew was in the neighborhood of 70 or 75 miles an hour. By the time I retired, of course, we had jets which were beginning to push the sound barrier. I flew some of the jets as the Phantom Jockey.

Q: You also had what's called a green card. Tell me about that.

Gallery: Well, I went through the instrument flying school and the green card entitled you to sign your own clearance, regardless of weather. It was a very highly prized thing and it wasn't too common either. I kept up this green card after I finished the school and I kept it up to date when I was at Glenview and also at San Juan. This entitles you to fly on instruments in any kind of weather, so it's up to you to decide just whether you want to go or not.

Q: After all that flying, your flying now is confined in a sense to the tractor, is it?
(The interviewer found Admiral Gallery riding his tractor-mower and cutting grass on what appears to be acres of lawn.)

Gallery: Yes, I haven't done any flying at all since I retired. I figure I used up all my luck while I was on active duty.

Q: Tell me about your writing career. I know you were involved in writing while you were on active duty, but I think you've done a great deal more since, haven't you?

Gallery: Yes. I got started when I was towing that submarine back from Cape Blanco in Africa, and I knew that I had the hell of a story at the end of the tow line there and I also knew that I would not be able to talk about it to anybody, including any ghost writer when I got back. So I thought, well, I'll try to write it up myself. I did and when we got in to port I turned my story in to ComInch, and ComInch promptly stuck it in a top secret place until the war was over. Then he took it out and sent it up to The Saturday Evening Post and The Saturday Evening Post took it. Well, how much luckier can you get, on your very first attempt at writing you make The Saturday Evening Post. So that's how I got started.

I went on from that to writing something about Iceland. Then after that - this was the time of the big B-36 fracas and the unification battle was on - I had a couple of pieces about unification in The Saturday Evening Post. The Post liked them but the Secretary of Defense didn't like them. The Secretary of Defense at that time was Louis Johnson and he and I didn't get along at all.

I branched out from that into writing fictional stories for The Post.

After I retired I combined a lot of my fictional stories into one book, which I called Now Hear This. It's thirteen different stories but they're all about the same character and they all occur in the same place, the same ship.

Q: Sort of Hornblower stories?

Gallery: Maybe. After Now Hear This, I wrote Eight Bells, which was my autobiography. This is an interesting sidelight. This is my autobiography. Now, you know, the Bureau of Personnel, when new books come out they have a board that reads them and decides that they'll buy certain ones and others they won't for ships' libraries. Their decision on Eight Bells was "this is not suitable for Navy libraries." Well, I think to turn down a rear admiral's autobiography on the grounds that it's not suitable for naval libraries is the same thing as a cardinal in the Catholic Church getting his book on the Index!

Q: Yes!

Gallery: But that's what happened, because in it I told about some of my battles with the Secretary of Defense and also with the Secretary of the Navy and what I thought about them. Then I published an article called "If This Be Treason" in Collier's, and Mr. Matthews, Secretary of the Navy, thought it was treason and said so in so many words.

Q: Let me read it onto the record, will you?

Gallery: Yes.

Q: It's from the Secretary of the Navy to Rear Admiral Daniel V. Gallery, dated 10 January 1950:

Subject: Your Proposed Article Entitled "If This Be Treason"

1. A draft of an article entitled "If This Be Treason" written by you and intended for publication has been received and examined.

2. This proposed article I consider to be not only inflammatory and inaccurate but contemptuous of and disrespectful to both the Secretary of Defense and to me. Its publication would constitute conduct prejudicial to the good order

and discipline of the Navy.

> Francis B. Matthews

Gallery: Incidentally, you know what, that "conduct prejudicial to the good order and discipline" is a legal phrase which they use in the specifications for a court-martial.

Q: Yes, indeed. There's a letter also attached dated January 18, 1950 to Rear Admiral Daniel V. Gallery from Ernest J. King and it's addressed "My dear Dan."

"I have read and re-read that article which you wrote in <u>Collier's</u> for the issue of January 11 entitled 'If That Be Treason,' in which you put your cards on the table, indeed.

I must say that your article was well written and I hope that most people will read and re-read it because you tell the truth, at least as I see it. The time has come for people to understand that a proper officer does not like to be made a mere yes-man otherwise, as you have said, the police state is close at hand.

Thanking you for your good work,

> Faithfully yours,
> Ernest J. King"

Quite in contrast with Secretary Matthews!

Gallery: Yes.

Now, let's see, I wrote Eight Bells, then my next three or four were fiction. Stand By to Start Engines was another collection of short stories, but all involving the same characters. Then I wrote The Brink, which was I guess you might say my first bona fide novel.

Along about that time the Pueblo was captured and I wrote "The Pueblo Incident", which was a description of the Pueblo case, in which I took a very dim view of Bucher's conduct.

After that I had two more books, Captain Fatso -

Q: That's a very humorous book.

Gallery: Yes - and Aweigh Boilers, which is another book about Captain Fatso. I have three books on Captain Fatso.

Q: How did you happen to get off into the realm of fiction?

Gallery: Well, fiction is easier to write than a serious book because you don't have to do a lot of research. I say I did the research, my forty years in the Navy.

You can just write it off the top of your head.

Q: Providing you can write and providing you have a sense of humor.
Well, I hope you continue writing. Are you doing anything now?

Gallery: I'm toying with the idea of another book right now.

Q: Who is your publisher?

Gallery: Norton has published five of my books and Doubleday two of them, Morrow one and Regnery one. That's nine altogether.

Q: Would you give me a footnote on the development of missiles and their use in the Navy? You were in at the very beginning, the early experiments with missiles.

Gallery: I don't know what to say about them, except that there are missiles in existence now capable of wiping out life on the earth. The Polaris submarines and their missiles are capable of wiping out a country like Russia.

Q: In your early work with missiles, was this sort of thing dreamed of? I mean development to this extent?

Gallery: Well, we had had the atom bomb. We didn't visualize these 25 megaton things that we've got now. We were dealing in kilotons then. Even so, one bomb one city.

Q: Well, it's been a fascinating career and it's spread over a tremendous area of development in different fields, and how fortunate you are to be able to utilize some of this experience and this knowledge in writing, making it available to others.

Gallery: Yes.

APPENDIX

How would *you* behave if you were questioned under torture by the Reds? Do we ask too much of U.S. fighting men who are taken prisoner? Here is a startling, controversial proposal from a hard-boiled admiral, who believes he has the solution to a tragic dilemma and says

We Can Baffle the Brainwashers!

By REAR ADMIRAL D. V. GALLERY, USN

The author

THE treatment of American prisoners by the Reds in the Korean war poses the free nations an evil problem: "What can we do about the communists' hellish brainwashing technique for torturing 'confessions' out of prisoners of war?"

This inhuman method for tampering with men's minds and souls defies all laws of God or man. It lays bare the frightful difference between our Western civilization and the godless creed of communism. The Reds used it ruthlessly on American prisoners of war in Korea, treating our men like laboratory rats in a diabolical scientific experiment.

A number of these men, through fear of being tortured to death, gave lip service to the Red creed or signed obviously false "germ-warfare confessions." Now some of them are being court-martialed or disgraced for cowardice and collaboration with the enemy.

This is happening in a country which let victory in Korea slip through its fingers because of fear—fear that we might touch off World War III, and thus get hurt ourselves. We try our soldiers for cowardice—after a war which we didn't have the guts to win!

There is an uneasy feeling in the land about these POW trials. But the trials are just a small, messy piece of the whole big problem—the piece least worthy of public sympathy. The real problem concerns the many other prisoners who took everything the Red devils could do to them and didn't break. Before we can live in good conscience with those 3800 men the Reds let come back alive, we Americans have got to face this problem honestly and courageously.

(The opinions expressed in this article are the private ones of the writer and are not to be construed as official or reflecting the views of the Navy Department or of the naval service at large.)

Perhaps, if we wanted to, we could even forget the past, avoid looking our 3800 ex-POW's in the eye, and just sweep the whole thing under the rug. But the future and the boys who haven't been captured yet make this problem cry out to heaven for solution.

I have no sympathy whatever for a prisoner who squealed on his buddies or who sold them out for his own benefit. We should throw the book at him and disgrace him. I have much sympathy for those who, under torture, gave the Reds "military information" of the kind we broadcast to the four winds in our magazines and newspapers. I understand and feel sorry for those who signed germ-warfare confessions or broadcast phony peace appeals. But the ones for whom I am really sorry are the boys who clammed up and took it, refusing to sign anything.

To be brutally frank about it, these lads accomplished nothing by their heroism. It certainly didn't bring the United States military victory. It didn't stop the Reds from winning a smashing propaganda victory in the Orient. Through the Big Lie technique they convinced the Chinese and many gullible neutrals that we were actually using germ warfare. Now our lads who held out against hellish tortures find public sympathy going to those who broke. The only good that came of their heroic resistance to brainwashing is the internal satisfaction which they themselves will feel from now on. For the rest of their lives they can look themselves in the eye when they shave in the morning and say, "Well, soldier, you took it."

As an American I am very proud of these men. But as an American I'm ashamed of the position we put them in. This must never happen again. We must fix it so that no prisoner will ever again have to endure torture to preserve the good standing of the United States before the other free nations or will feel that an absurd confession extorted from him may be held against him if he survives.

General Dean, captured early in the Korean war, is a brave man. He got the Congressional Medal of Honor. He was never actually brainwashed, but when threatened with it, he decided the only way he could prevent the Reds from getting what they wanted out of him was suicide.

We've got to find some better choice for the defenders of our freedoms than torture, suicide or disgrace. That's all we give them now by our rigid insistence on the Geneva Convention formula. Our

Jan. 26, 1954: Three of the American POW's who refused repatriation—Pvt. James Veneras, Pfc. Richard Tenneson and Pfc. Samuel Hawkins—wait to be interviewed by newsmen at Panmunjom, Korea.

Cardinal Josef Mindszenty at his 1949 treason trial before a "people's court" in Red Hungary.

A communist "China Photo Service" picture of Marine Col. Frank Schwable, which purports to show him "confessing" to germ-warfare charges.

military regulations say that a prisoner may state his "name, rank and serial number," but beyond that he must clam up and endure whatever ungodly tortures the communist devils inflict on him. As far as the regulations go, anything more can bring public disgrace when and if he ever gets home. This harsh rule is uncivilized, un-American and stupid. It plays right into the communists' hands, lending credibility to the few confessions which they are able to extort by brainwashing.

All through the whole stinking record of brainwashing in Korea, one thing stands out like a sore thumb: What the Reds were after was propaganda, such as germ-warfare confessions and peace appeals. Any military information they picked up was an incidental by-product. Propaganda was their real pay dirt, and it was to work this lode that they used brainwashing.

Let's lay this evil thing on the page here and look at it, if your stomach is strong enough. Brainwashing is a devilish new process developed by the Russians through experiments on dogs and rats. Their psychologist, Pavlov, found that by regimenting and frustrating animals, and by constant repetition of a set of circumstances, such as ringing a bell just before feeding them, he could "condition their reflexes" so that the animal's mouth would water every time a bell rang. He discovered he could blunt their natural instincts and replace them with "conditioned reflexes" of his own choosing.

The Red brainwashers follow this same technique. They first reduce their victim to about the status of a dog or rat. They make you live in solitary filth, deprived of all human contacts. They strip you of all human dignity and deny you food and sleep till you are nearly, but not quite, dead. Torture is used judiciously, with clinical skill. Time drags out into eternity, where you are alone with your thoughts. You become a borderline case between a human being and a rat struggling to stay alive. Then constant interminable repetition of their ideas erodes your brain. Your senses of proportion and values get distorted. Eventually your natural instincts may be replaced, like the rat's, by conditioned reflexes.

(Continued on Page 94)

Maj. Gen. William Dean, just after repatriation. When threatened with brainwashing, he came near suicide.

This Red propaganda photo is titled, "U.S. Germ War Participants Repatriated." The author suggests we tell the world that, hereafter, captured GI's will "confess" to any and all charges.

WE CAN BAFFLE THE BRAINWASHERS!

(Continued from Page 21)

If they keep hammering at you that it is raining outside, sooner or later you may believe it. Sometimes, if your torturers are competent, skillful operators, they can eventually lead you out into bright sunshine and you will still think it's raining. A confused and beaten man can even be convinced that the Reds are right—that we are the aggressors and they are the peace lovers.

How much of this torture anyone can take without breaking depends entirely on the individual. No one who hasn't gone through the wringer himself can say where his own breaking point might be. Those who have been broken are the only ones who know. They are the only real experts on brainwashing on this side of the Iron Curtain. Those who took it without breaking are charitable toward those who did. They say, "Maybe they bent those other men harder than they did me."

The men who suffer most from brainwashing are the highest type of men our civilization produces. The Reds apply pressure to both your brain and body till one or the other breaks. If it's the brain, you confess. If it's the body, you die. The better man you are, the worse you get it.

Strong physical specimens of only average will power get off easy, because they crack soon, before their bodies are irreparably damaged. If you are weak physically, but strong-willed, that's not so bad—you will die fairly quickly. But if you are strong both physically and mentally, God help you. Occasionally the Reds lose patience with a strong will and quit, so the torturers can work on more productive subjects. But communist patience is difficult to exhaust.

Men have always been willing to die for a principle. The history of martyrdom from the early Christian days down to the present time proves that simple fear of death cannot break a strong man's will or make him deny his faith. But months of a bare, animal-like existence, with the safe haven of death near, but always just out of reach—that is something new and diabolically different. There is abundant proof that many brave men, perfectly willing to face sudden death, cannot hold out indefinitely against this fiendish half-death. In any large group there will always be a percentage, not cowards or weaklings, but just average human beings, who will eventually break and "confess" to whatever the fiends demand. When this happens, the heroic resistance of those who held out becomes a gesture of ghastly futility.

To show that the communists break even strong characters by brainwashing, I cite three very different types of strong men they have broken. The first is Cardinal Mindszenty. Cardinals are not weak characters—they certainly are not afraid to die. But Mindszenty "confessed" in open court to what the Reds wanted. Another strong type is Colonel Schwable, United States Marine Corps. Schwable, a flier of twenty-four years' experience, was universally regarded as an outstanding officer in a corps noted for its officers. Fliers are not afraid to die. But Schwable signed a false confession to "germ warfare." A third type is the Reds' own commissars. Commissars are unprincipled and ruthless, but they are strong, tough characters. They have to be. The Reds break them too. In the Moscow purge trials the deposed commissars sang like canary birds!

We should know by now that we aren't all heroes and what happened in Korea will happen again. We had better quit burying our heads in the sand and do something to counter it. I don't think the American people want to keep on offering their sons the choice of suicide or disgrace.

There is a simple way out of this grim mess, if we have enough vision and imagination to use it. Recall what happened in the case of Cardinal Mindszenty. Living among the Reds and knowing their methods, he foresaw they might break him, and disavowed his "confession" before he was even arrested. His solemn disavowal and prediction of what they would do to him was published to the world before his confession. The confession, when it came as predicted, was useless for propaganda purposes. Its publication backfired on the Reds and made them look stupid. This points the way for us on the brainwashing problem.

Suppose the President of the United States were to issue an Executive Order to the armed forces right now, telling our men that, if captured by the Reds, they may sign any document the communists want them to or appear on radio or TV programs and deliver any script the Reds hand them. Tell them they can confess that the United States poisoned Lenin and Stalin; they can call the President a capitalist, warmongering dog of Wall Street; they can broadcast peace appeals, agree to settle behind the Iron Curtain when the war is over, and sign long-term leases on houses in Moscow. Give the Reds anything they want for propaganda purposes and defy them to use it!

This order would be transmitted to the United Nations with a blistering statement explaining why we had to do it, and serving notice that hereafter statements of our prisoners, made to the enemy, would be a bunch of fairy stories. This statement should be accompanied by several hundred affidavits from our men who went through the brainwashing process that will stink to high heaven. Properly publicized, this could put the Reds on the defensive in their cold war with the free world. It would spotlight the inhuman atrocities of the communists and bring out the grim fact that the Geneva Convention, which has more or less governed the warfare of civilized nations in the past, is useless in dealing with godless fiends like the communists. We should hammer home, on the Voice of America and at the United Nations, that this convention worked after a fashion in World Wars I and II, when we were fighting human beings of more or less our own background and type. Even the Japs believed in God and a future life. But now that our enemies are ruthless, godless devils, we have to release our men from Geneva Convention restrictions.

World-wide publication of such an Executive Order would make the Reds look ridiculous on this side of the Iron Curtain when and if they attempted to use brainwash "confessions" in the future. It would leave no further motive for brainwashing except sadism. I'm sure there are many sadists in the communist ranks, but maybe the perverted sexual urges of Red interrogators will be satisfied sooner if our boys agree with their obviously false accusations.

Some people object that our disavowal won't penetrate the Iron Curtain, so the Reds could use these confessions to convince their own people that we were committing atrocities. They don't need them for that. They can manufacture confessions for the benefit of their own slave peoples—make them up out of whole cloth. They need "confessions" to convince gullible neutrals, and our disavowal will reach and impress them.

As long as we stick to the rules we had in Korea, the communist devils, bound by no rules of God or man, will make us look stupid. What chance has a lone GI prisoner against a battery of brainwashing communists? Look at the record in Korea. By sticking to our outmoded Geneva Convention rule under impossible conditions, we let the Reds persuade millions that we had flouted all civilized rules and used germ warfare.

The germ-warfare charge was an easy bill of goods to sell in Korea and China, where many diseases are epidemic. What could be simpler than to blame them on United States germ bombs, producing many actual victims of the diseases to prove it? They didn't need actual confessions to do this; they could have manufactured the signatures as well as the confessions. Behind the Iron Curtain it made no difference whether Colonel Schwable actually wrote his confession or whether the commissars simply announced that he did. Slave peoples have no choice but to believe.

Their reason for wanting actual confessions was so they could publicize them, transmitting them to the United Nations, to raise doubts in the minds of our timid neutral friends. They succeeded in this diabolically well. They used the very organization which the free nations have set up to preserve peace and foster understanding among nations to spread lies about us and stir up distrust and hate. From a purely technical point of view, as a propaganda operation, it was a slick job.

In propaganda the Reds were always slick and we were clumsy. Through brainwashing they were able to broadcast peace appeals by our men. What kind of appeals did we broadcast? We pleaded with twenty-two of our men who had actually transferred allegiance to the Reds, "Come home, all is forgiven." When one of them did come home, we court-martialed him—just as the Reds predicted we would! How stupid can we get? That blunder will be a windfall to the communists' propaganda for many years.

We missed one marvelous chance to make bums out of the Reds during the long-winded truce negotiations in Korea. One of the issues on the exchange of prisoners was whether we would force thousands of unwilling former Reds to go home. There were 70,000 prisoners who wanted to go back, and 100,000 who didn't. We haggled for months about this.

We could have stopped the haggling and made the Reds look foolish very simply. Suppose we had secretly loaded all the 70,000 confirmed Reds into our amphibious fleet, landed them behind the communist lines and just turned the whole rabble loose. Then we announce to the world, and the Chinese in particular, "These rats are so worthless that we are giving them back to you for nothing. For negotiating purposes they aren't even worth one American prisoner; you can have them free." Think of the loss of face this would involve in the Orient for every one of those 70,000. The Reds, carried away by their own germ-warfare lies, might have taken drastic antiseptic precautions!

But we can't think like that. We follow the book; our actions are unimaginative and perfectly predictable. The Reds know it, and use us as if they owned us. They sold the Big Lie on United States germ warfare to the whole Orient.

Many people ask, "Why did the Reds go to so much trouble extracting confessions which they didn't need in China or Korea, and conducting classes in POW camps to 'educate' our men?" Some of our prisoners have a startling answer to this question. They say maybe the Reds were looking ten or twenty years ahead, hoping for another depression in the United States.

What you have drilled into your brain in a POW camp stays with you the rest of your life. Maybe you don't believe it for a long time. But ten or fifteen years later, if what the Reds predict about a depression comes true, then maybe seeds the Reds planted will take root and sprout. This may seem farfetched to us who live from year to year. But it isn't to Asiatics, who look at centuries as we do at months. It is typical of the difference between our propaganda and theirs.

Moralists may object to my proposal, on the ground that it is always wrong to tell a lie. A lie is a deliberate false statement, made with intent to

"It's been an hour already—how long do these demonstrations usually last?"

deceive someone who has a right to demand the truth. What I am proposing would be done with intent to deceive nobody. It would be done to prevent colossal deceptions such as the germ-warfare lie, which all the Reds in China still believe. It would be given worldwide publicity beforehand, so the Reds would look foolish if they verified our predictions by producing this kind of confession. Past performance indicates they are far from stupid in propaganda. They are much smarter than we are.

Besides, the only truthful answers which the Reds have a right to demand from our prisoners are "name, rank and serial number." If you insist that we must deal with devils on a moral basis, you can say, "This is a moral twist to the Big Lie technique." Call it the "sea of lies" if you want—lies that are harmless because we predict, identify and authorize them; daring the enemy to use them.

Others object that this proposal would open the floodgates for a lot of military information. I don't believe it. In the first place, the Reds have access, through our magazines and newspapers, to more authentic military information on technical subjects than they can digest. The public-information branches of all three services compete with one another for press space, and the easiest way to sell a feature article on a military subject is to tell an editor, "This hasn't been released before; you're getting a scoop." If I were in the Red Navy, I could easily make a reputation in Moscow as the greatest spy in history. I would get assigned to Washington as naval attaché and simply do a rewrite job on stuff I can buy on any newsstand.

In regard to tactical information, no prisoner knows anything that can really affect the outcome of World War III. That will be decided by natural resources, production capacity and things that the communists know all about from the atomic scientist, Doctor Fuchs and others like him. To protect their own front-line units, most of our prisoners only have to keep their mouths shut for about a week. After that, tactical dispositions on the front have changed so that they can spill all they know without affecting the outcome of even a local battle one way or the other. Those who know things that might affect the future of the war, such as future tactical or strategic plans, must not be allowed to subject themselves to the risk of capture.

It makes fine reading in the newspapers when General MacArthur wades ashore right behind the first assault wave or General Patton barges into an enemy-held town in the lead tank. But it's a badly miscalculated risk when we permit them to do this. Sure, it's good for morale—of a limited number of front-line troops, and also of the generals concerned. But think of the shot in the arm it would be to enemy morale if they were captured. And think of the really vital military information their capture would jeopardize.

MacArthur is a brave man, and so was Patton. But they were never brainwashed. No one can say just how much they could have taken before they broke. Major tools of the brainwashing process are degradation and humiliation. Obviously the higher a prisoner's rank, the further you can degrade him, and the easier it is to humiliate him. We say you must tell "name, rank and serial number," but if I were ever captured, those are the three items I would do my damnedest to conceal. Maybe I could give my rank as RADM and claim it meant "radioman."

All our ideas about military security require a drastic overhaul. Our GI's and all our citizens know too much. We should tighten up on military information and pass it out only on a "need-to-know" basis. This would help to protect our prisoners as well as our secrets, because you can't betray a secret if you don't know it.

We might also revise our ideas on what constitutes "collaboration with the enemy" in the light of what goes on back here in these United States. Back here, during the Korean snafu, Peress stopped a Senate committee cold, when they asked him if he was a communist, by invoking the Fifth Amendment. Soon thereafter he was promoted to major and given an honorable discharge. When our captured soldiers are being brainwashed, there is no law this side of hell they can invoke. All they can do now to stop the torture is to "confess"—or die.

Our present policy of dealing with some of our own prisoners of war is a windfall to the communists. Compare how we treat a brainwashed GI with the treatment guaranteed by the Constitution even for criminals. A soldier who had an obviously false propaganda confession tortured out of him can be tried by court-martial for giving "aid and comfort to the enemy." A criminal who has a true confession beaten out of him by the police goes scot-free if he can prove that he was forced to tell the truth about an actual crime. This is one of the American rights that our soldier was defending when he got captured. I wonder how he feels when a false con-

(Continued on Page 98)

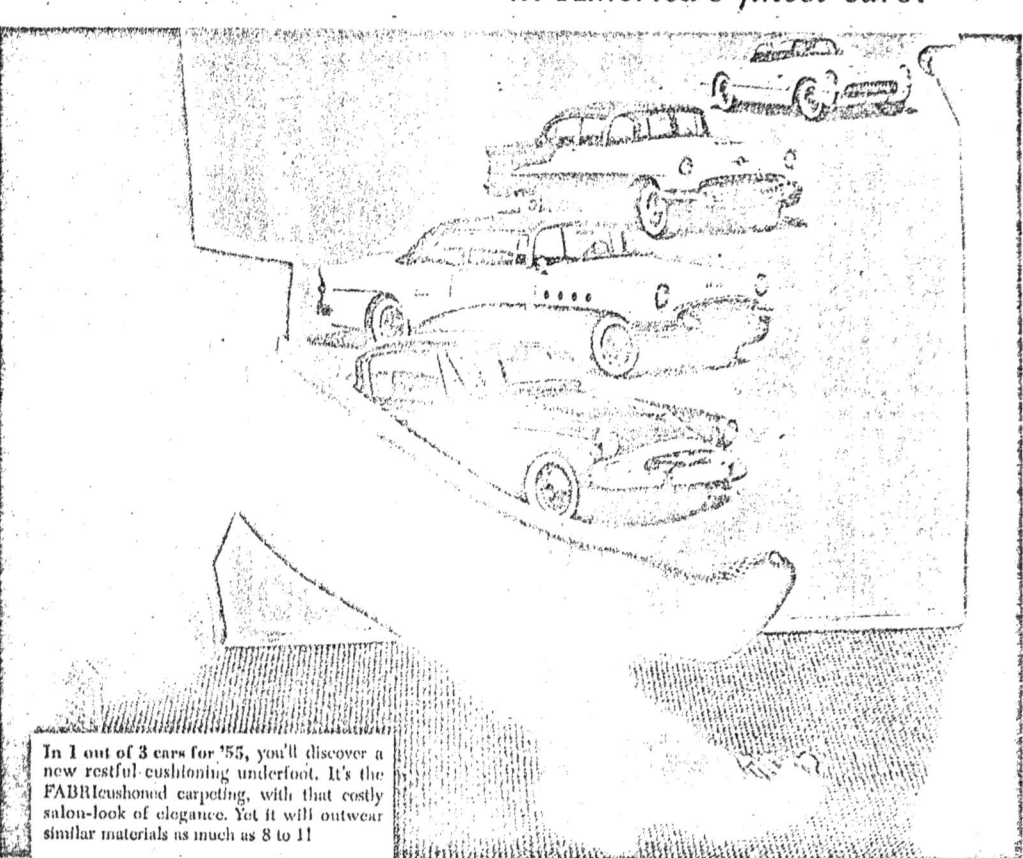

WHETHER YOU BRUSH YOUR TEETH JUST ONCE, TWICE, OR 3 TIMES A DAY...

Colgate Dental Cream Gives The Surest Protection ALL DAY LONG!

Because Only New Colgate Dental Cream —Of All Leading Toothpastes—Contains GARDOL* To Stop Bad Breath Instantly.. Guard Against Tooth Decay Longer!

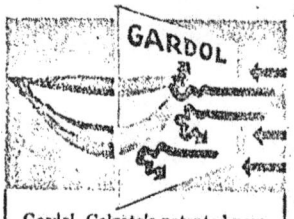

Gardol, Colgate's patented new decay-fighter, forms an invisible shield around your teeth. You can't feel it, taste it, or see it— but Gardol's protection won't rinse off or wear off all day. That's why Colgate's—the only leading toothpaste to contain Gardol—gives the *surest* protection ever offered by any toothpaste!

Your dentist will tell you how often you should brush your teeth. But whether that's once, twice, or three times a day, be sure you use New Colgate Dental Cream with Gardol! Colgate's stops bad breath *instantly* in 7 out of 10 cases that originate in the mouth! Fights tooth decay 12 hours or more! In fact, clinical tests showed the greatest reduction in tooth decay in toothpaste history!

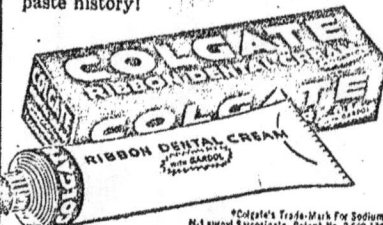

*Colgate's Trade-Mark For Sodium N-Lauroyl Sarcosinate. Patent No. 2,542,170

Every Time You Use It...New Colgate Dental Cream
CLEANS YOUR BREATH *while it* GUARDS YOUR TEETH!

(Continued from Page 95) fession, extorted by the Reds, is produced before a United States military court composed of men who have never even seen the Reds face to face.

We didn't even brief our men consistently in Korea on what to say if captured. The Army, Navy, Air Force and Marines all had their own ideas on this question, and different units of the same service differed. The briefings given to our men going into battle varied all the way from zero to carte-blanche advice: "Spill anything you know; they know it too." The "name, rank and serial number" briefing was Stateside stuff that you got from people who knew they would never be captured. Some units avoided any briefing whatever on this question "because telling the men about communist tortures would be bad for morale."

I agree that frank briefing on brainwashing, for men who may have to face it, probably won't make them very happy. But that's no excuse for burying our heads in the sand and trying to ignore it.

When all the brainwashers want is agreement with their ideas, their job is relatively simple. They just put the heat on you until you sign what they want. Then the interrogator has documentary proof for his commissar that he is a shrewd operator. But if they go after military information, the job is much more difficult. They have to evaluate what you say, cross-check it against known facts, and make up their own minds. Their "conditioned-reflex" technique doesn't cover this. They may have to go back to the dogs and rats in their laboratories and conduct further experiments to find out how they can tell when the animal is behaving "truthfully" rather than the way they have conditioned it to act.

Some of our expert interrogators and psychologists say there is no use trying to deceive expert interrogators; you just have to clam up and refuse to answer. If you lie, they will find you out. Our boys who went through brainwashing say that on military information, they could get away with evasive or false answers. But when the Reds demand a "yes" answer to a propaganda question, you either give it to them or else.

We can't give our boys shots so they won't be hurt when tortured, get weak when starved or become dopey from lack of sleep. But maybe we can save them from enduring these tortures rather than confess to obvious lies. The least we can do is to assure them that whatever they say or do under these circumstances will not help the enemy, because we have disavowed it ahead of time. We can thus relieve their minds of the gnawing fear that what they say will be held against them when they get home. All our boys to whom I have talked agree that was perhaps the worst fear that haunted them during their ordeals. That is one dragon we could slay forever with an Executive Order.

This is one of those things on which it seems we have nothing to lose and a lot to gain. The communists, even if they continue their brainwashing, can't treat our men any worse than they have. At the very least, we will insure that none of our men endures the ordeal of brainwashing through fear of being stigmatized as a traitor if he signs an obvious fairy tale.

General Dean, in his book, makes this very significant statement: "One of the first things I noticed was that these people were much more anxious to have me say what they wanted me to say than to extract any really new or useful information. Pressure on me was greatest to agree to perfectly obvious falsities." Many other ex-prisoners agree that the only real heat put on them was to extract false confessions for propaganda purposes.

Our present military regulations are designed to protect military information, and all evidence shows that the communists don't use brainwashing to get military information; they use it to get propaganda material. Why should they bother trying to extract military information from our prisoners? In a battle to conquer mankind with an idea, it doesn't pay off. If an expert interrogator pries the location of your artillery battery out of a prisoner, they may destroy or capture your battery. But under present conditions, if he pries a false confession out of him, he may capture the minds of 300,000,000 Asiatic people.

There is no power on this side of hell that can prevent the Reds from brain-

★ ★ ★ ★ ★ ★ ★ ★ ★

LINES ON A HALF-PAINTED HOUSE
By Maxine W. Kumin

In summer, beach and billows beckon;
And in between, you dab a speck on.

In autumn, who feels dutiful?
The foliage is beautiful.

In winter, little can be done;
The brush will freeze, the nose will run.

Spring's the time! The perfect instant!
And fortunately, two months distant.

★ ★ ★ ★ ★ ★ ★ ★ ★

washing and breaking a certain number of our men. But we can cut the ground out from under them for propaganda purposes, and thus destroy the usefulness of brainwash confessions. We might spare our men a lot of heroic but utterly futile resistance to torture in the future, and insure that never again will the communist devils be able to make us look as bad as they made us look in Korea.

To leave the solution of this problem in military hands isn't fair to anyone concerned, including the much-maligned military brass. Military men have a Spartan code of ethics of which they are justly proud, and the American people rightly expect them to live up to it. If we leave this problem in their hands, we can expect a Spartan solution, all wrapped up in a neat little ball of military wax, such as "name, rank and serial number," for foot soldiers and the bombardier of a B-47 alike.

The problem is only partly military and it is much too big for any such pat solution as that. We have to educate the American people to realize that we aren't playing a game any more, a game that can be run by gentlemen's agreements and international pacts. We are in a life-and-death struggle with a godless system bent on world domination, a system which regards human dignity as a zero quantity.

Against the brainwashers the Geneva Convention is as obsolete as the TNT bomb. It is our duty to the future defenders of our freedoms to find a better answer to it.   **THE END**

Index for
Series of Interviews with
Rear Admiral Daniel V. Gallery
U. S. Navy (Retired)

ANTILLES DEFENSE COMMAND: one of three commands assumed by Gallery (1956), p. 176; p. 190.

AZORES: p. 75-6; p. 84.

BUREAU OF AERONAUTICS: p. 27; p. 30; p. 36.

BUREAU OF ORDNANCE: Gallery as officer in charge of aviation, p. 30; contracts for Norden Bomb sight, p. 31-34; expansion of the program, p. 35ff; gallery's tour of duty in London for the Bureau, p. 37-38.

BURKE, Admiral Arleigh: p.181.

CAPE CANAVERAL: Gallery member of committee to select the missile launching site, p. 135; p. 137.

CARIBBEAN SEA FRONTIER: Gallery takes command on Dec. 6, 1956, p. 175 ff; also becomes Comdr. 10th Naval District, p. 176.

CASAIS, Palbo: p. 201-2.

CASTRO: incident involving kidnapping of thirty U. S. sailors returning in bus to Guantanamo, p. 179 ff.

SS CERAMIC: British passenger steamship, p. 84 ff.

CHURCHILL, Sir Winston: Visit to Puerto Rico, p. 182-4.

COLLIERS MAGAZINE: Gallery article on Unification and dismissal of Denfeld, p. 132.

COM CAR DIV SIX (1951): Gallery's flagship was CORAL SEA with Sixth Fleet, p. 155 ff; account of the search for missing fliers from the CORAL SEA, p. 158-162.

DANIELS, Worth Bagley: p. 8-12.

DONA FELICIA: Mayoress of San Juan, p. 185-6.

DOYLE, Admiral Austin K.: Commander, Naval Air Training, p. 173-4.

GALLERY, RADM Daniel V.: personal data , p. 1-3; father's decision to send 3 sons to Naval Academy, p. 3-4; Gallery's early duty assignments, p. 15-16; his decision to be an aviator, p. 20; makes flag rank, p. 127; retirement for physical disability (1960), p. 203; his career as a writer p. 206-212;

GALLERY MEMORANDUM: p. 141 ff; (see copy of Memorandum in appendix).

USS GUADALCANAL (CVE): Gallery goes to Oregon to commission Kaiser Class jeep carrier, p. 63 ff; simulated attack on Panama canal, p. 72; episode involving German SS refueling off Azores, p. 75-6; night flying, p. 77-91; the provocation, p. 79 ff; U-515, p. 81 ff; U-68 p. 89 ff; p. 100; Gallery's final cruise on the GUADALCANAL, p. 121-2; U-505 her capture, p. 97 ff; p. 109 ff; p. 111; post-war history of U-505, p. 115-121.

GUIDED MISSILES: Gallery becomes the first Assistant CNO for Guided Missiles, p. 128; p. 134-5; Gallery fires a V-2 off the MIDWAY, p. 135-9; the forerunner of POLARIS, p. 147-9.

USS HANCOCK - CV: Gallery takes command in Pacific (1945), p. 125-7.

HENCKE, Oberlieutenant Werner: skipper of U-515, p. 81 ff.

HUNTER-KILLER FORCE, ATLANTIC (1952): Gallery takes command, p. 162-4.

USS IDAHO: P. 18-21; p. 30.

ICELAND: Gallery becomes Commanding Officer, Fleet Air Base (Jan. 1942), p. 38 ff; duty on BPYs operating off Iceland, p. 40-1; radar equipment on PBYs p. 53 ff; Squadron bags its first German Submarine, p. 55 ff.

JOHNSON, The Hon. Louis: Sec-Def - tries to control writing of articles on unification, p. 129 ff; p. 142; p. 147.

KAISER CLASS CARRIERS: p. 64-5.

KING, Fleet Admiral E.J.: a student at Pensacola, p. 22-24; p. 124; p. 132-3; his letter to Gallery in approval of the article - "If This Be Treason", p. 209.

LITTLE LEAGUE: Gallery organizes LITTLE LEAGUE teams throughout Puerto Rico, p. 199-200.

LOCH ERNE SEAPLANE BASE: Gallery becomes Commanding Officer (1941), p. 37.

MATTHEWS, Francis P. - Sec Nav: his reaction to the Gallery article in Colliers - "If this be Treason", p. 132-4; his letter to Gallery, p. 208.

USS MISSION BAY - CVE: p. 72-3.

MUNOZ-MARIN, The Hon. Luis: Governor of Puerto Rico, p. 183; p. 186; p. 188-9.

MURMANSK CONVOYS: PQ 17, p. 47-50.

U. S. NAVAL ACADEMY: entrance to the Academy (Aug. 1917), p. 6-15; athletics, p. 7-14; summer cruises, p. 12.

NAVAL AIR RESERVE TRAINING COMMAND (1952-55): Gallery takes command at Glenview, Illinois, p. 165 ff; Gallery has temporary duty as Commander, 9th Naval District (simultaneously), p. 171-2.

NAVAL AVIATION: Gallery's first interest, p. 20; Pensacola, p. 21; duty with torpedo squadron (1927-8), p. 25-7; Gallery goes back to Pensacola as an instructor (1930-31), p. 27; Gallery spends three years in aviation ordnance, p. 28-29;

See also: entries under USS GUADALCANAL: LOCH ERNE: ICELAND: REYKJAVIK: COMCARDIV 6; NAVAL AIR RESERVE TRAINING.

NAVY LEAGUE: Chapter in San Juan flourished with Gallery, p. 190 ff.

NIXON, The Hon. Richard M.: As Vice President inspects Reserve Training Command at Santa Ana, p. 169-170; his visit to Venezuela (1957), p. 177-8.

NORDEN BOMB SIGHT: p. 31-34.

USS NORTON SOUND: converted to rocket launching ship for experimental purposes, p. 127; p. 151.

PEARSON, Drew: Prints the Gallery Memorandum on Unification and the Air Force, p. 142 ff.

PENSACOLA: see entries under: NAVAL AVIATION: ADMIRAL KING.

USS PILLSBURY - DD: p. 98; p. 100.

USS PITTSBURG: Gallery has duty on her in the Mediterranean, p. 17-18.

POST GRADUATE SCHOOL: p. 28-9.

R.A.F. - Iceland: p. 42 ff; plan for attack on the German BB TIRPITZ, P. 59.

REYKJAVIK, ICELAND: Headquarters (1942-4) U. S. Navy Fleet Air Base, p. 41-63.

SATURDAY EVENING POST: Gallery writes for magazine, p. 130-1; his first story p. 206.

SEABEES: p. 42.

SEAPLANES: See entries under: LOCH ERNE: ICELAND.

SHERMAN, Admiral Forrest: his letter of admonition to Gallery for Coller article, p. 133-4.

STEEL BAND: Gallery imports steel drums for Navy Band in San Juan, p. 193 ff; visit to the World's Fair in Brussels, p. 196-7; the ensemble becomes known as ADMIRAL DAN'S PANDEMONIACS, p. 197; plays for Pablo Casals, p. 201-2; p. 204.

SUBMARINE WARFARE - Atlantic: p. 45 ff.

SULLIVAN, The Hon. John: Secretary of Navy - his reaction to the Gallery memorandum, p. 142-3.

TEL-AVIV: p. 160-2.

TENTH FLEET - SS DATA: p. 74-6.

BB TIRPITZ (German): p. 47-48; p. 58-9.

TORPEDOES: Gallery's description of their use in exercises of Torpedo Squadron (1927), p. 25-7.

TURKEY: USS PITTSBURGH at Contantinople in time of Kemel Ataturk, p. 17-18.

U-68 (German): p. 89 ff.

U-515 (German); p. 81 ff.

U-505 (German): her capture, p. 97 ff; significance of capture of German code books, p. 109 ff; towed into Bermuda, p. 111; her post-war history, p. 115-121.

UNIFICATION: Gallery writes for SATURDAY EVENING POST on unification, p. 129 ff; the Gallery MEMORANDUM, p. 141 ff (see copy of Memo in Appendix).

VIEQUES: p. 187.

von BRAUN, Dr. Werner: p. 152.

VS SQUADRON FOUR: Gallery on duty with this Scouting Squadron on the LANGLEY, RANGER, SARATOGA and LEXINGTON, p. 29 ff.

www.ingramcontent.com/pod-product-compliance
Lightning Source LLC
Chambersburg PA
CBHW080614170426
43209CB00007B/1427